Your Life is Now!

MARLENE GEORGE

Sandi,
Live a joyful life
Marlene.

TRAFFORD

Printed in Victoria, Canada

National Library of Canada Cataloguing in Publication Data

A cataloguing record for this book that includes the U.S. Library of Congress Classification number, the Library of Congress Call number and the Dewey Decimal cataloguing code is available from the National Library of Canada. The complete cataloguing record can be obtained from the National Library's online database at: www.nlc-bnc.ca/amicus/index-e.html

ISBN 1-4120-2311-4

TRAFFORD

This book was published *on-demand* in cooperation with Trafford Publishing.
On-demand publishing is a unique process and service of making a book available for retail sale to the public taking advantage of on-demand manufacturing and Internet marketing. **On-demand publishing** includes promotions, retail sales, manufacturing, order fulfilment, accounting and collecting royalties on behalf of the author.

Suite 6E, 2333 Government St., Victoria, B.C. V8T 4P4, CANADA
Phone 250-383-6864 Toll-free 1-888-232-4444 (Canada & US)
Fax 250-383-6804 E-mail sales@trafford.com
Web site www.trafford.com TRAFFORD PUBLISHING IS A DIVISION OF TRAFFORD HOLDINGS LTD.
Trafford Catalogue #04-0139 www.trafford.com/robots/04-0139.html

10 9 8 7 6 5 4 3 2

Table of contents

Dedication and Acknowledgments

To my mother and late father, for their love and support, and from whom I learned so much.

My husband and son, for their support and patience during the writing of this book. I love you both dearly. You are two of my greatest life teachers.

Other members of my family who in many different ways support my work.

My clients and students who taught me so much and inspired me to write this book.

Those clients who so willingly offered their stories, so that the reader will be inspired to implement some of the information in this book to bring more joy into their lives.

My many teachers, some mentioned and others not mentioned, who through their teachings I learned so much about myself.

Anne Lynn Henry for her Foreword and help during the writing of this book.

My editorial consultant, Martha D. Humphreys, for all her skillful editing, ideas and attention that helped to expand the vision of this book. And for living up to her mission of keeping the book as close to my words as possible.

Sharry Wilson for her skillful proofing and willingness to meet my request so that I could forward the book to the publisher.

Sharon Richards for the beautiful book cover and CD covers.

All those at Trafford Publishing who contributed to the final completion of this book.

To anyone else who offered their time and attention to support the completion of this book.

Foreword

When I first met Marlene George, I was at a very low point in my life. After 25 years together and two children, I was going through a very difficult divorce and the break down of the marriage devastated me emotionally, physically and financially. My psychiatrist recommended hospitalization. I couldn't eat or sleep. I was having difficulty concentrating, working and looking after my family.

At that time, I made a decision. I wanted to get whole again as soon as I could, but I did not know how. While shopping at a local drugstore, I found myself looking at the magazine rack. I saw a periodical I'd never noticed before called *Divorce Magazine*. I picked it up and thumbed through it. It had listings of agencies and services for people like me.

I bought the magazine, took it home and called every number that I thought could possibly help me.

I left a lot of messages on answering machines. One of the people who called me back was a man named Dave Clark. He was a manager for a group of psychologists who provided weekend seminars. The price was too steep for my circumstances at the time, but I could tell he was a very compassionate and caring person. I told him about my situation.

He said, "You need Marlene George."

"I need Marlene George?" I replied.

He repeated, "You need Marlene George. I know her and she has wonderful success helping people in difficult situations. You should call her. Here's her number."

I called her immediately. She was wonderfully accommodating. She had an affordable workshop that would meet my needs. Unfortunately, I already had a conflicting engagement. She suggested a creative way to solve the conflict which enabled me to attend her workshop.

Her workshop transformed me. I learned techniques, dealt with runaway emotions and gained insights about myself that have dramatically altered the course, quality and enjoyment of my life. And I was not the only one. I saw her do amazing work with all of the people in the workshop. Some were survivors of rape, incest and other serious traumas.

One of the other participants said to me, "A workshop with Marlene is equivalent to years of therapy."

Since then, my daughters and I have had the privilege of attending several enlightening sessions with Marlene. I see a tremendous change in myself I feel like a different person. Or, as my younger daughter said, "You're more yourself, Mom."

In my journey to find meaning and answers in my life, I've read many books, listened to countless tapes and attended dozens of seminars. They have all helped me in varying degrees, some tremendously. But that first session with Marlene, along with her subsequent expert coaching led to my biggest breakthroughs and quickest progress.

I feel extremely fortunate that I was sent the people and tools I needed to help me. I am eternally grateful to the one who helped me first, Marlene George.

Marlene glows with inner and outer beauty. She radiates warmth, vitality and healing. As you will see from this book, she is also very down to earth, practical and honest.

Marlene's skill as an outstanding stress therapist, and Reiki and Therapeutic Touch teacher are well known in her community. I am delighted that she has written this book. It greatly widens the circle of people she can help.

If you follow the steps and exercises Marlene sets out in the nine chapters that follow, I am sure that your life will be enhanced immeasurably. I also recommend her inspirational compact discs on Health, Happiness and Harmony to speed your progress.

All the best to you on your journey of self-discovery!

Anna Lynn Henry

Chapter One

Your Life IS NOW!
Now is the Time to Live the Life You Want!

The Present Principle
Joyous Living Skill #1: Your life is Now, Now is the time to live it!

This work is a product of my journey from ignorance to enlightenment. From childhood, through adolescence and into adulthood, I struggled with many issues common to all of us, and some which were mine alone to understand. Through the right circumstances, and my openness to the universe, eventually I learned a way of life that has benefited me, and those who have attended my workshops and counseling sessions and who have come to me for treatment. My work is a product of my lessons, both personal and professional. In addition, I've studied and listened and learned from other teachers the universe has brought into my life. My clients and those who have attended my workshops have requested this book for years Until recently, I felt I was not ready to write it. Then, after a combination of several starts, synchronicity and courage, I have taken the material and distilled it into my teachings, including visualizations and exercises which will help you discover the same degree of joyous living as I do on a daily basis. Included are my **Nine Principles For Joyous Living**, one for every area of your life, to help you get happy and stay that way. After reading this work, you will understand the importance of your feelings, your acceptance of them, and their application to your overall well-being. You need not take my word for it, instead take a leap of faith and do the exercises, practice the visualizations and see what happens.

My Story

Born on July 27, 1942 in Cape Town, South Africa; my memories of my early childhood are vague. This is not unusual, for studies show most people do not have cognitive memories prior to age 3. I looked relatively happy in my childhood pictures. I am the middle of three sisters who were born 10 months apart. My sisters and I had happy times together, we loved to sing and talk and we had no secrets. As with most of my clients, my life had its ups and downs, its triumphs and disappointments, all the elements which create the adult I grew to become. For instance, in my first year of school I was at the top of the class. Then in the following year I failed and was held back. Although I don't remember why I was not promoted, I do remember how sad and ashamed I felt. From that year forward, school for me seemed to be a struggle. It was not because I did not like school, but learning for me was not as easy as it was for my sister, a future school teacher.

As with most men of his generation, my father distanced himself from me and my two sisters. He was a good provider, but he did not know how to express his love for us. I do not recall him ever telling me he loved me. On the other hand, my mother provided plenty of attention as she attended to her duties fulfilling our daily needs in spite of her challenging marriage. My father was a very angry man. Because he had to fend for himself from a very early age, he was angry with the world. There was constant tension in our household as my mother tried to make up for the kindness that was missing from my father's early life. Rightly or wrongly, I found myself in the middle. Taking on their emotional pain, I was the surrogate husband for my mother and the surrogate wife to my father. Caretaking their feelings left no room for my own. From my adult perspective, I recognize that my role in my family was the second major event in my life where I felt held back.

During that time, dancing was my relief and my salvation. I took classes in ballet and modern dance from age 4 to 16 years old. Apparently I had the talent and the desire to become a professional dancer. Unfortunately, my parents did not have the resources to send me abroad for formal training. Again, I felt held back. Unable to fulfill my dream of becoming a professional dancer, I turned my creativity elsewhere. I left school at 16, and became a hairdresser. When I turned 17, my mother set me up in my own hairdressing salon which I successfully ran for the next 7 years. In addition to the satisfaction of being self-supporting, I benefited from learning a lot about my clients' concerns, problems, successes and failures. Those years broadened my perspective on the world and my place in it.

Unknown to my parents, I was sexually abused during my early teens. Because of the shame and feelings of powerlessness, sexual abuse creates control issues with the victims. Many women attempt to control their lives through overeating, effectively padding their bodies in an attempt to protect themselves from further abuse. I chose the opposite path. My efforts to control my world lead to anorexia when I was 17 years of age. This was my subconscious's way of putting myself on hold again. I did not want to evolve into having a rounded female body. This lasted until I was 23 years old when I married my husband who I met when I was 17 years old.

Currently, we have been married 38 years. As with most couples, the first years are the most difficult as husband and wife discover who they really are after the first blush of attraction and commitment. Our first years were further complicated because of my trust issues around men. In addition to the effects of my sexual abuse, my mother always said "Men cannot be trusted," perhaps echoing my grandmother who said "Men are only after one thing," meaning sex. This legacy again placed me on hold, as I feared giving my heart fully to my husband. It was during this period I found my first yoga book. I started practicing and realized the gift of relaxation I was given with this knowledge.

Our son was born two years after our marriage. Because of the apartheid system in South Africa, we decided to immigrate to Canada in order to provide a better life for our son, David. It was a major leap of faith for our marriage, since hairdressing was my only skill and my husband also had no official trade. What were we thinking? We immigrated to Canada with only $500.00 in our pocket and I knew my days as a hairdresser were over. Instead, I worked in varying fields including commerce, foreign exchange, stocks and bonds, real estate and finally at the university. This experience expanded the interpersonal skills I had acquired in my hairdressing business. In addition, during my real estate career I was introduced to Bob Proctor, Wallace D. Waddle, Claude Bristol, Anthony Robbins and Thomas Troward, all proponents of the human potential movement with the emphasis on manifesting what you want and creating your own reality. During these years, I took business and psychology courses while pursuing a Fine Arts program at York University. I began to study the Alternative Health field. Through the Fine Arts program at the university, I began to work on myself by applying the knowledge from the psychology classes. My expression was improved through theatre classes. Simultaneously I worked on my own self-healing journey.

In the early 80s I knew it was time for me to work on myself. I never had physical pain in my body, but I had many emotional issues that demanded my attention. A friend of mine told me about Therapeutic Touch, and how it was a great avenue for healing oneself. I enrolled, and the gift that I received from one of the teachers was her insistence that we not only learn Therapeutic Touch to help heal others but to also be willing to heal ourselves. I learned Reiki and later CranioSacral Therapy. Another teacher introduced Holotropic Breath work, discovered by Stan Groff. This powerful yet gentle modality has helped me in so many ways to transform myself and become a happier person. It was through this work that I was introduced to Jacquelyn Small, who taught breath work and other seminars which focused on Unconditional Love in Relationships. It was at one of her workshops that I met Gary Zukav, who was responsible for "The Seat of the Soul." Then I was introduced to Sandra Ray's work on the concept of the mirror in our lives when dealing with our relationships. Rather than accept our feelings, we project them onto others in order to cope with them. Once we acknowledge this process we are able to deal with our feelings in a more accepting and positive manner. Another aspect of mirroring is expressed in Abraham Hicks's teachings which explain how we attract what we project. In order to attract more of what we want, we need to project what we want rather than what we don't want. This is also known as the Law Of Attraction. During this period and into the 1990s I studied the works of Paul Solomon, Thomas Keller, Louise Hay, Charles Fillmore, Norman Vincent Peale, Carl Jung, Marianne Williamson, Catherine Ponder, Edgar Casey, Bernie Segal, Louise Hay as well as Abraham Hicks.

Finally, one of my teachers asked me, "Marlene, when will it be enough? How any more courses do you need to take to begin your work?"

That day I made another important decision in my life; I was ready to share with people what I had learned.

I started my first Healing Circle with 4 people teaching about learning to love and value ourselves. It is said we teach what we need to learn. It started with my fear.

The first time I remember feeling fear was a few years after coming to Canada. I was in my late thirties and I started to ask myself: "Who am I? Is this all there is? There has got to be more to life than being married, a mother, wife and going to work." Happily I fulfilled these roles, but something was missing, and I wanted more. That is when I went to college and took business, marketing and courses in human relations. Then, I enrolled in a Fine Arts degree program and studied theatre, music, dance, psychology, and general arts courses This new focus along with the following teaching moved me forward and provided me with the skills to have and live the happy life I enjoy today. Still, something was missing. I was educating myself on the outside, but there was work to be done on the inside as well. I felt as soon as I discovered what "it" was I could help others, too.

I started to listened to tapes and watch videos on the work of Anthony Robbins, Wallace D. Waddle, Bob Proctor's teachings on Napoleon Hill, Thomas Trowad's work and many, many real estate teachers (this list is too long to record) all talking about setting goals, attracting money, about attitude and how our thoughts produce our results.

These teachings became a part of my practice: setting clear goals and helping my clients stay focused on their vision with regard to money and also to have faith that what they are wanting will come. Visualizations and thinking in the positive is encouraged as well as applying appreciation in all areas of their lives. We also work toward accepting the connection between their mental and physical form and how to believe before they receive.

In early 1990, I was attracted to the Unity Church which teaches a new thought process. The congregation was nurtured and developed by Charles and Myrtle Fillmore. There were discussions around the universal laws including the Law of Attraction, Law of Increase, Law of Thinking, Law of Receiving, Law of Supply and Law of Non-Resistance, just to mention a few. They all confirmed what I always believed and felt which is that my life is a reflection of my thoughts and feelings and that under every pain is an emotional component in which the body follows the mind. Therefore, if dis-ease shows up in our bodies it is a result of our thinking.

My clients are encouraged to be aware of their thoughts with regard to what they are wanting in their lives. They are shown how the body follows their thinking with regard to the dis-ease they have created in their lives. This includes their thoughts around their family, forgiveness and all types of relationship and money challenges and how they feel about themselves.

I was also introduced to "The Course in Miracles," which focuses on relationships and Catherine Ponder's "The Millionaires of the Bible" series, which focuses on creating and attracting money. "The Course in Miracles" helps my clients understand their relationship with themselves and others, and how fear holds them back and creates challenges for them and their other relationships. In order for them to have a better relationship with themselves or with others they need to transform themselves form the inside by changing how they feel about these connections. Other influences help them to understand their connection to their source and their understanding that we are loving beings and that we are here to express that love to ourselves and others.

Catherine Ponder's work affirms the power of believing. Our lack of trust in ourselves and our source holds us away from all that we desire I help them see how their resistant thoughts and feelings are keeping them separated from the things that they want and to help them think and feel prosperity in all areas of their lives.

With John Bradshaw's teachings, I help my clients to heal their past family challenges and this work mostly includes forgiveness. Louise Hay's and Bernie Segal's teachings are primarily used when the person has a health challenge. I help them understand how the body created the illness due to their thinking and how by thinking more positively about the body, it will heal. That visualization and affirmations are also a powerful way for them to change how they feel and see their bodies. How the power of the spoken word can create the miracle they want.

Having attended many workshops and lectures by Paul Solomon and Thomas Keller, I apply their methods to help my clients focus on ways to heal and how we think and feel about ourselves and others. Through these teachings I help them to see how they think about themselves; which may include their low self-esteem, not feeling worthy, not loving themselves and their unhealthy relationships with themselves and other.

I feel that I was very fortunate because when I got into the alternative healing field my teachers stressed that it is very important to heal ourselves. What they meant was that many who come into this profession are only interested in learning these techniques because they want to heal others and they are not interested in looking at themselves. I always stress to my students that they have to be willing to heal themselves, too. "Healer heal thyself, Physician heal thyself, the therapy can only go as far as the therapist has gone." This creates a powerful healer.

Therapeutic Touch was discovered by Dolores Krieger, Ph.D., R.N. This is a non-invasive technique which uses the flow of energy through the palms of the practitioner and effectively helps relax, reduce anxiety, reduce pain and supports the body's own natural healing process. When I went to learn this process I was very healthy physically, but I knew I had some emotional healing to do, and I had heard that this modality would help me. The teacher was Patrick Mahoney who then introduced me to Djuna Harper, another Therapeutic Touch teacher who did other forms of transformation work which included the Holotropic Breath work. This process was created by Dr. Stan Groff.

I continued my healing with Jacquelyn Small through the Holotropic Breathing process. This modality combines powerful breathing with evocative music, art, creative self-expression, focused bodywork, and group processing done in a safe healing environment. It unblocks and brings new energy and balance to the body, thoughts and emotions. It releases fear, denial and anxieties, freeing one from patterns and programs that are no longer useful to our personal growth. We rediscover our magnificence and renew our commitment to live our lives with more peace, joy, harmony and love. She also taught about love and relationships.

In my practice, I use Therapeutic Touch to help bring my clients' bodies and minds to a relaxed and sometimes less anxious state so that their mind can then encourage the body's own natural ability to heal I have also taught thousands over the years how to use this modality on themselves and others. Many of them expressed how this modality has transformed them in positive useful ways.

The Holotropic Breathing is a powerful tool that many clients have used to heal relationships, health, self-esteem, worthiness and money challenges. Every session for them is different and they continue to feel more and more empowered. They feel healthier, clearer, more focused and passionate about what is before them, even if it was not all clear to them at the time.

Carl Jung's work taught me about the shadow side of myself. This includes the side of me that I tried to deny and hide from myself and others, and the aspects of myself that I was not happy with. My clients see how what they have been feeling and thinking is actually the dark, bad parts of them and how this has had power over them and has affected their lives in many ways for the worse. When they give themselves permission to let go of the blame and guilt they start to appreciate and love themselves more and become happier, healthier and more successful.

Reiki was another energy healing process that helped me release all types of mental and emotional issues. Discovered in the 1800s by Dr Mikao Usui, besides healing the physical challenges it also works on the underlying causes of the problem. It is also a powerful tool towards Spiritual Growth and Evolution, through releasing old energy patterns and allowing the dynamic acceptance on Unconditional Love. This leads us towards the development of our own Intuitive Guidance and a Transformation of Consciousness. Through this treatment, besides feeling more relaxed, my clients allow themselves to release blockages in their bodies, emotions and their mental thinking. This transformation results in them feeling healthier and more in harmony with their lives. Students who came to learn how to use this tool on themselves and others have said over the years that Reiki has changed them and their lives for the better.

CranioSacral Therapy was another avenue that I learned to help bolster resistance to dis-ease and transform emotional imbalances. This tool is used in my treatments especially on those who have had accidents and have head, back or neck injuries. Those who have learned this skill are using it and incorporating it in their treatments with the other.

Peter Inman incorporated many transformational techniques, some of which included bone and muscle manipulation to readjust the body, psychic surgery and the powerful invocations which will be given in Chapter 7 which discusses health. His work also included transformational work and consultations. Besides all the energy work that Peter taught me, he also taught body adjustments through manipulation similar to some chiropractic adjustments. Another part of his teaching besides loving oneself was the releasing of negative thoughts and negative entities through ritual clearing.

I was then introduced to The Abraham Teachings. These teachings confirmed all the other teachings and added for me a further dimension. They bring together all the other teachings in a simple and clear message that is easy to understand and incorporate into our lives depending on how committed we are to our goals, aspirations, and spiritual growth.

Each of these areas required a leap of faith on my part to truly benefit from the information they offered. I made that leap of faith, and if you are willing to do the same, you too, can benefit. Please follow the chapters in the order they are presented as they lead you through the process of becoming who you really are and who you really want to be.

1) My story: my life and learning illustrates the importance of living in the Now, The Present Principle. The past is behind us, the future is ahead of us, and all we can truly experience is today. So, it's important to make the most of it today and every day.

2) Higher Self: once we accept the importance of the present, we realize that we do not have to live our lives alone. Each of us has an inner guidance system which will steer us on the path of least resistance if we allow it. When there are pitfalls and challenges, it is our higher self telling us to examine our feelings

about the situation. Once we feel good about something we can progress, knowing it is the right thing for us at this time.

3) Self-esteem: We learn that most of our self-image is determined by others' perceptions of who we are, or who we should be. Take a leap of faith in my process and free yourself from others' expectations. Instead, rely on your own sound judgment.

4) Fear: This reaction is your higher self telling you that you are pursuing something that you don't want instead of something that you do want. Recognize it for the catalyst for change it is, and welcome it into your life in order to change your life for the better.

5) Relationships: the first relationship to improve is the one with yourself. Learn to accept and love yourself and you will attract the relationships you want in your life.

6) Forgiveness: The most important process to free yourself from negativity in your life, by getting past those people you perceived as bringing negativity to our lives. Once you forgive yourself, the process expands to include others.

7) Health: your body follows your mind. The Seven Chakras are physical manifestations of your spiritual and emotional health.

8) Wealth: The practical application of the Universal Law of Attraction

9) Forever Young: Eternal Spiritual Youth can be yours by surrendering your expectations and enjoying your powerful present!

A Joyous Living Skill accompanies each chapter. Take your time and enjoy the journey.

Chapter TWO

Higher Self

Joyous Living Skill #2: Stay Joyful, trust your Higher Self to Guide you to the things you want!

The following personal story expresses the gift we receive when we stay connected with our higher self. A gift beyond measure, our higher self provides the courage, the faith and the strength to deal with whatever life hands us if we remember to connect with our spirit for guidance. The process is our point of power, the present. Every minute of every day, our higher self is available to us.

My Story

As a young child I remember standing at the window gazing up at the moon. I knew there was magic and mystery out there even though I could not describe it. I knew I was a part of all that and always would be. I also knew there was no separation between me and this amazing glow in the sky I somehow knew I was a part of the all and that no matter what, I would always be fine.

My grandmother and mother also gave me that feeling. They both made me believe and feel that I could have whatever I wanted for myself, and that no matter what I will go through, I will be guided if I trust and let how I feel direct me. I learned through staying happy and positive, I will fulfill my dreams. I now know that this was the most important thing my elders taught me and I appreciate them for this.

After the war period, in the late 1940s, we had to cover our windows to conceal the inside house light and stand in line for rations; all of this for me was one big adventure. Even though I overheard many sorrowful stories about the war, I seemed to be able to stay happy.

Years later, the announcement came of the new government taking over. There was so much discussion and concern among the adults about this new apartheid system. But somehow I knew I would be OK. It was a feeling that I had and just trusted.

My sisters and I would have so much fun playing, singing and laughing. Even though I loved being with them, I had my own quiet places I would go to, like out in the fields and around animals. This, I believe, was my way of reconnecting with my source and to remind myself who I am. As the years went along I found less and less opportunity to take this precious time with myself and my higher self.

In my early teens, I did volunteer work with my mother. We visited the people who were less fortunate than our family. I surprised myself in that I never felt sorry for them. Somehow I sensed that all was well, that they were exactly where they needed to be. I loved to visit them, but had no concern or judgment as to how they were living their lives.

My first two years at school were great. I was among the top students in the class. This made me feel good. Then when I went to the third class, I failed and was held back for another year. I remember how bad I felt. I felt shamed, stupid and less than useful. This was when I lost a little faith in myself and in the world. School after that was always a struggle. I was a B student but worked hard to maintain this average. I know now that my failing the grade, and the feelings and beliefs I attached to that event continued with me into my later years.

At that time, I believed that people put me on hold, but I now know through all the teachings I have studied, that I placed myself on hold. In retrospect I see this all clearly now. It was just a belief I bought into and which continued with me into my adult life.

Before we immigrated to Canada, I shared my life-long dream of visiting Australia with my husband. He supported my wish even though we did not have the means to fulfill my dream then. We left South Africa for England and then to Canada when I was 26 and still had that unfailing faith that we would be fine. That whatever I needed I would always be able to receive. I had no knowledge of the Universal Laws at the time.

During all these years I never gave up my dream to visit Australia. In 1986 I was working as a real estate agent. The market was very slow and I felt that although I loved what I was doing, something seemed to be incomplete for me with regard to my career. I also got tired and more depressed about taking all the action I was doing to generate business. I decided that this was the perfect time to fulfill that childhood dream, which was to visit Australia. I also included New Zealand to visit since I had friends there. I traveled by myself, and stayed with lovely people in Australia. I spent many days by myself, lying on the beautiful Australian beaches. It was during this time by myself that I again found my way back to me and my source. I decided that when I returned I was going to leave real estate and start my own business in the health field. This was the end of 1989. We sold our condominium and cottage and bought our dream home where I established my business. As usual, the timing was perfect.

As I reflect on my life story I see the gift of my higher self's guidance. Take a moment and reflect on your life's story. When you were connected to your higher self, things went easily. If you distanced yourself through denial, fear or ignorance your life reflected that estrangement. Again, the time is now, your life is now, so learn all you can about your personal spiritual guidance system in order to stop getting what you don't want and start getting what you do want.

What Is Your Higher Self?

That universal creative power, our inner guidance, that unlimited supply of energy that is available to all of us. We just have to open to it. That universal power that we all are an extension of, with no beginning no ending. And we all have the infinite power of the universe available to us. There are no concessions. All we need to do is to ask for what we want, trust what we want is on its way and stay happy. Like the baby in the mother's womb, once the impregnation takes place and the mother is healthy and happily looking forward to the birth and trusting that everything she wants around the pregnancy will develop and unfold perfectly. She can trust that her wishes will be granted. Another example of this is when the bulbs of perennial plants are in the ground, we expect them to flourish year after year, and they do. And those monarch butterflies find their way every year when they migrate to their destination. Each of us has the potential to be who we want to be, to have what we want to have, and create the lives we dream of simply by accessing the universal creative power available to all of us.

Each of us has access to this infinite power; and there are as many ways to become connected to our universal source as there are people on the planet. At birth, our original state was happiness. In order to connect to the universal creative power, or our higher self, we need to return to our original state of bliss. Some people use prayer, others use meditation. The source can be found in music, exercise, and art. Any form of creativity returns us to our source. In short, just do anything that feels good and we will always be fully connected to our source. In the early stages of my life, most of the time I was happy, and therefore fully connected to that inner guidance. My first realization of being disconnected from my source was my reaction to being held back at school. My reaction stemmed from my beliefs and perceptions surrounding the event, which had nothing to do with my source. I now know that I had developed some resistance to life. Events placed my life on hold.

What I have learned through the teachings is that no matter how far off course I may be, all I have to do when I feel I am being placed on hold is to ask for what I now want in positive terms, feel good about myself and trust that my request has been heard, and then joyously wait for the outcome.

Ken's Story

"At age 53, I understand that "healing" is a life-long process. Along the way we meet many teachers, guides and friends who enable us to speed up the process, to "shorten time by collapsing it" as A Course in Miracles calls it. One of my teachers, to whom I am very grateful, is Marlene George. Marlene led me to many new insights about myself and God.

One of the real breakthroughs in my spiritual growth came one afternoon as I lay on Marlene's wonderful therapeutic waterbed with built-in sound system and described my memory of an incident from my infant years. As she worked on my body with therapeutic touch I conjured up a vivid picture of myself lying in my crib and crying uncontrollably. My mother, frustrated I suppose with my crying and her inability to control it, had put on her coat and told me she was leaving. (I learned later in life that HER mother used this same threat to manipulate my mother's behavior and the behavior of her siblings when they were young, hiding in the woodshed to give them "a little scare.")

Needless to say, this technique was anything but consoling to a tiny child and I recalled and experienced the terror with great intensity under Marlene's healing touch. Then, as I lay there in my childhood crib, a great sense of calm came over me and I became aware that there was an angel there with me in my crib assuring me without words that I was safe and loved. It was an amazing sensation of peace and well-being. And it was the most profound lesson of life: <u>that we are never alone and we can never be abandoned because our Creator is always close at hand if</u>

<u>we only lay down our blocks to the awareness of Love's presence</u>. For this insight, Marlene, I am truly thankful." K.E.

Evelyn's Story

"Like Ken, I recall a comforting image when events challenge me. Whether in my business life or personal life, I keep going back to an image I used as a child for solace. I see myself on top of the moon and I am looking down on the planet. I find this gives me a bigger perspective. This image brings me back to reality and takes me beyond the insignificant nitpicking things we can so easily get drawn into like judgment and guilt. Then, I remember the good times. And I use a lot of appreciating and allowing, then relax and let the good things happen." E.G.

Ways To Access Your Higher Self

Higher-self Visualization:

1) When Are You Enough?

Find a comfortable place to lie down or sit, somewhere where you will not be disturbed. You may want to cover yourself. Now, take in a long, slow, deep breath. On the exhalation feel the tension in the body leaving you. Take a few more slow breaths in and out. With every breath feel yourself relaxing more and more. If there are any emotions floating around, breathe them out with every breath. Notice your thoughts, allow them to just pass you by as if watching a TV screen. Just notice. Do not try to change the thoughts. Take another long, deep breath, and on the exhalation, let go of any final tension you may be holding. Feel all the muscles let go and melt into the object you are resting your body against.

Focus on your head and face area and if you feel any tension in that area, just let that go. Any frowning or tension around the jaw, relax more and more. Relax any tension behind the eyes. Any tension around the throat let that go. Notice the shoulders and down through the arms and down into the wrist and hands, relax more and more. Take another long, deep breath in, and then breathe it out, as you feel the body soften and relax more and more. Now focus on the stomach area and all the way to the back muscles, all around the ribcage area. Release more and more. Continue down into the pelvic area and into the buttocks, relax. Down into the thighs, the calves, the ankles and the feet, letting go more and more. Check one more time by scanning the body again. If there are any emotions floating around, give yourself permission to set that aside for now. Take in another deep, long breath. Exhale as you allow the body to relax even more.

Take yourself to a place where you feel safe. It may be the beach; maybe you can hear the ocean breezes and the lapping of the waves as you smell the ocean air. Feel the sun on your body as you watch the clouds roll by. In the distance you hear the sound of children's voices.

Maybe you are out in a garden or a park. You are sitting or strolling in the beautiful park with its gardens. You smell the scents of the different flowers and the wild herbs. You can feel the grass under your feet. You are feeling so peaceful, relaxed, yet alert now. Make yourself comfortable. Maybe you are seeing yourself leaning up against a tree or standing under a waterfall or lying in the ocean. Know that this is the perfect place for you to be now. This is your time and you...just be.

Take some time to think about things or people in your life you appreciate. It may be your family or your friends or it may be people at your work. You may want to appreciate yourself, the life you live. Nature or anything you can think of that you would like to appreciate. Bring all your sense into the experience.

Now give yourself permission to invite your inner being into this visualization with you. Feel the connection of merging more and more with your inner being. Feel the appreciation your inner being feels for you Allow yourself to bask in those feelings of your higher self's love for you.

Feel the merging taking place. Notice how the body softens, and how the senses feel more heightened.

Now ask your higher self this question: "WHEN AM I ENOUGH REGARDING RELATIONSHIPS?" Wait for the response. Listen for the answer.

You may want to jot down your answer now, or you may decide to write it down later.

Ask your higher self to help you reach that place of feeling complete within yourself with regards to relationships.

2) Now ask your higher self: "WHEN AM I ENOUGH REGARDING MONEY?"

You may see an image, hear a word/words or feel the answer.

You may want to ask for guidance for ways to create more money, to feel contented in the meantime while the money comes and or to feel happy and complete with what you have today, knowing that if you created it before, you can create and attract more.

3) Now ask your higher self: "WHEN AM I ENOUGH WITH REGARD TO MY WORK?"

   Wait for the reply.

4) Now ask your higher self: "WHEN AM I ENOUGH REGARDING MY HEALTH?"

   Listen, hear or feel the answers which may be ways to improve your health and well-being.

5) Ask you higher self to provide you with any other information that will help you to move forward. Listen for the answer.

Now with this wonderful feeling of connection with your inner being see yourself now going through your day. See how easily everything unfolds. Situation after situation, all going and unfolding exactly as you wanted. You are surprised how smooth everything is manifesting. Doors are opening, paths are clearing and mountains are moving to bring to you what you have been asking for. You are amazed how everything is happening with such ease. You feel happy, healthy, and abundant in all areas of your life. You feel invisible and ready to conquer the world.

You feel joyful and happy while all that you have been asking for starts to manifest itself.

Tell your inner being that this is how you would always like to feel about your life. Make it your intention that if you stray too far away from these feelings of who you really are, that you will ask your inner being to give you a sign, a nudge, or anything safe and light to get your attention so that you can bring yourself back to the true essence of who you are.

You tell your higher self you want to continue to be happy, joyful, and appreciative and more forgiving of yourself and others. Also, you would like to create more of these opportunities to connect and feel closer to your source.

Take in a long, full breath as you feel a sense of peace and well-being. Breathe out and take in another long, slow breath. When you are ready, become fully present. Go over to a mirror and look into your eyes. Feel your connection to your inner being. Feel the love and appreciation beaming back at you. Stay there as long as you wish, enjoying your closer connection with your higher self.

(These visualizations and others in this book by Marlene George are available on CD.) www.marlenegeorge.com <http://www.marlenegeorgecom>

You can download and listen to a segment of the 3 CDs: Health, Happiness and Harmony.

Exercises

1) Write down the answers you received.

2) Draw the images you may have seen.

3) Write what you saw with regards to the doors and paths opening and bringing you what you have been asking for.

4) Write down the promise you made yourself to stay happy no matter what.

5) Write down what you felt when you looked into your inner being's eyes.

6) Write down what it felt like to feel more connected to your inner being.

7) Find pictures in magazines to place in a box (treasure box) that represent the feelings and images you saw or felt, or place these words and images on your collage or in your scrapbook.

8) Place some of the empowering words you received in places that you often see (i.e. the bathroom mirror).

9) Do some intending with the information you received. See yourself having fun in your relationships. Intend that this is what you want now and visualize yourself having fun with these people.

Finally, the important key is to have faith that the universe will deliver all that you want. It is about trusting, relaxing and knowing that what you asked for is on its way.

Follow these steps in the days to come:

1) When we are feeling happy, everything that we have been asking for is on its way to us. And when we are feeling negative we are holding what we want away from us.

2) Remember in those times when things are not going the way we want; it is during these times of discomfort and confusion that our desire for what we want needs to be much stronger. This is our opportunity to decide and ask for what we want.

3) Remember to find a place that feels good. In other words, it is most important that we feel happy so that we can attract what we want.

4) Identify what we want in the positive by rephrasing our words and thoughts so that we can attract more joy. Affirming is powerful.

Student comments

"Over the weekend the spirit was moving in me to write the new deputy warden and to my therapist about my case. I have been visualizing a move to a more peaceful and calmer institute. At lunchtime, today, I visualized meeting one of the staff who I hadn't seen for a month, and visualized handing two envelopes to her to deliver copies of my assessment to the deputy warden and the therapist. To my amazement I went to lunch and back but did not see the staff anywhere. On a gut feeling, I sensed I should turn a corner and look to the left of the building where she works. To my surprise, when I doubled back on the hunch, the staff member was standing there talking to another staff member! I approached them and provided the letters for delivery which she accepted without question. I was half expecting her to ask me to drop the envelopes in the internal mailbox, as mail delivery for inmates is definitely not part of an acting warden's job, especially in her lunch break!" E. G.

Synopsis

If we want to remain fully connected to our source we have to get happy and stay happy. Then everything we want will be delivered to us at the perfect time.

Your higher self will join us when we are appreciative and happy. We need to remind ourselves that we are more than the challenges in our lives, that we always have a choice of how we want to handle these problems. When we take a few breaths and refocus on the positive outcome of what we now want, answers and ideas will come streaming in.

chapter Three

Self-esteem, Self-worth

JOYOUS LIVING SKILL #3: STOP LOOKING INTO OTHERS' EYES FOR VALIDATION. THIS IS YOUR LIFE AND YOU GET TO CHOOSE HOW YOU WANT TO FEEL.

It has been my observation that most of us do not love ourselves enough. We do not feel good enough, we are self-critical, we feel less than, we are blameful, we feel fearful and guilty. This lack of self-esteem is a product of our upbringing. The beliefs and perceptions we hold about ourselves began in our childhood, and often were imposed upon us by our parents and others. Or we misunderstood or misinterpreted the signals we received during our childhood. In either case, the results are the same

For those of us with self-esteem issues, we have internalized and made what others said and thought about us our beliefs and attitudes. We took on their negative criticism and negative self talk and then lived our lives in accordance with these assumptions. So their negative self talk became our negative internal critic. We started to live our lives by looking into their eyes, and depending on what we perceived we saw in those glances, those looks dictated our day. This is not a judgment on our caretakers. They are acting from their pain, because many of them were not shown how to love themselves. So they, in turn, were also expressing what they learned from their parents and their peers. Many of my clients' insecurities dictate how they express themselves personally and professionally, and in their relationships. Some are very well educated, hold primary positions at the workplace, have all the money they want, but they are still unhappy. They have wealth and success and they are still not feeling satisfied that they have accomplished enough. They do not enjoy what they have manifested, because it never seems to be enough. They live a life of "When I accomplish this..." then I will be happy. Some will reach their goals, but still feel empty and do not fully enjoy what they have achieved. Their lives are a constant struggle dealing with the pressure that they place on themselves to achieve more. They are striving to create the perfect lives. But no matter how hard they try they do not reach their goal. Success seems to be just out of their reach. As a result, they are frustrated and feel less than. This restlessness stems from their upbringing where many of them were never encouraged and given guidance. Or in many cases the guidance given was very strict and confining They were never allowed to express their own individuality. They had to conform to their parents' needs or peer pressure of what others wanted them to become.

This is not to place blame on their caretakers because more than likely they had been brought up in a very strict environment themselves. Or in some cases some were left to fend for themselves. Their upbringing left many of these caretakers also feeling a lack of confidence and self- worth. Their behaviour then affected how they, in turn, treated their children.

Many of my clients constantly compare themselves unfavourably to others. They never feel fully satisfied because it was never enough for the others who they were trying to please. They are constantly striving to reach and fulfill standards that others have placed on them. Many of theses clients have not been aware of the undue pressure they have placed on themselves, trying to fulfill someone else's criteria. It has become evident to them that no amount of pushing and striving will change how they feel about themselves, never being good enough. Through our discussions many of them have become clearer that no matter how little or how much success they have accomplished, until they change how they feel about themselves, their lives will continue to feel like a struggle and they will not be as happy as they would like to be. In many cases they were never told by their parents or their peers that they were loved. They were not shown love, so they do not know what it is to love themselves. What we most want is to be loved and to love ourselves. But as long as this is not happening, we will never feel completely satisfied and happy. When we feel worthy and love ourselves, we will feel good about who we are. We will feel confident, secure, invincible, powerful, creative and loving, successful and happy.

Umberto's Story

Umberto's father set high standards for himself and his family His father was especially demanding on the sons. No matter how well they did in school it was never enough. If they came home with a B grade he demanded an A. No praise was given when they did well. The father lost his father at a very young age. What he most remembered about his father was his father's constant preaching about how important it is to have a good education. Because of Umberto's father's early death, there was no money to send him to college or university. Umberto had to leave school and go out to work to help his mother support the family. Umberto did any job he could find to earn money. Many times he felt he was being taken advantage of because of his limited education. He felt shamed and he had low self- esteem and he always felt less than the other employees. Umberto made a promise to himself that he would make sure that this would never happen to his children. He was going to make sure that they had a good education.

Umberto's father brought his insecurities into his relationship with his sons and expected them to accept and live in accordance to his dream and wishes for his sons. But this dogmatic attitude only stifled Umberto, which resulted in challenges for him in later life.

Parental abuse and neglect whether intentional or accidental through death or divorce can create self-image issues for their children. The other side of the coin are parents who are so fearful and anxious themselves they can not help but pass those fears on to their children, either by example or over involvement in their children's lives. Whatever the conditions, we must keep in mind that the parents chose their circumstances as much as did their children. The relationship was intended to be one of lessons taught and lessons learned as each member progresses along the path they've chosen.

Irina's Story

Irina grew up in a very controlled environment. Her family was concerned about her well-being, but their concern was displayed through fear. With this rigid and fearful upbringing Irina felt very insecure and anxious. Irina paid a lot of attention towards her mother. Her mother, in turn, did the same. So their relationship was one of both parties feeling smothered by the other.

Her mother constantly worried about money. Irina grew up listening and feeling her mother's fears and anxieties about finances. The fear her mother displayed was due to the mother's upbringing where she heard the same message from her parents. Her parents were always displaying or talking about lack around money. So Irina's mother brought all her insecurities about money into her marriage and then, in turn, imparted her feeling on the family.

Irina worried about all the family members. She became the primary caretaker in the home. She lived in fear all her young life, now expressing both her parents' constant anxious feelings.

Irina married, but that marriage failed, partly due to her concerns and feelings of lack around spending money. This caused dissension and much unpleasantness between her and her husband.

When I met her, she was very anxious, overwhelmed with the burdens and the negativity at home.

Through the sessions it became evident to Irina that she had to change her perceptions and beliefs about her family or nothing was going to change for her. She started to see how she was attracting this negative behaviour from them, because this is what she believed them to be. The more she felt negative towards her parents; they, in turn, verified and confirmed her thoughts. We talked about how negative she was about herself, her self- critic and self loathing. She did not feel she was attractive or good enough.

She also expressed that her dream was to one day have her own home. She knew that the move would help her to feel better, because she would be away from the negativity in her parents' home. But she also realized that if she did not change how she felt about them, she would be holding her self back from creating a happy life for herself. Although she moved away, she still held and felt all the memories and unhappy thoughts about their relationship.

She also realized that if she continued to feel resentful and angry toward them that she would attract other similar experiences from others. If her feelings about her family did not change, moving away from home was not enough to change her circumstances. She would have to change her beliefs and her attitude toward how she felt about them or else, the same cycle would start all over again. She knew that her thoughts and feelings would take her right back to what she no longer wanted in her life, especially with regard to judging herself and others.

Irina finally moved out of her parents' home and now lives in her own house.

The following is what she did to manifest her perfect home:

1) She wrote many appreciative things about them and told them how much she appreciated them.

2) She would write lists of things she appreciated about life in general.

3) She also wrote lists of the things she appreciated about herself.

4) When things in the home became too overwhelming she would either leave the house or go to her room and find things do to distract her. She would find something to focus on to feel good.

5) She would revisit her goals and visualize herself enjoying the things on her list.

6) Sometimes she would write a story about how she wanted her future to be.

7) Most importantly, she focused and thought more about what she wanted in these relationships and made sure that she felt good in the meantime until she saw evidence of positive changes.

If we do not feel good about ourselves and do not believe we are worthy to have whatever it is we want, no amount of action will change things for us. We need to change our thinking and how we are feeling about ourselves.

Frances' Story

Frances was sexually abused at the age of three. She did not feel protected by her parents when the incident occurred. Frances grew up in a home where there was a lot of illness. Her two grandmothers and her grandfather were both ill. All her mother's time was devoted to Frances' grandparents. Through this Frances felt neglected. The sexual abuse happened again, but this time by someone else. Now Frances knows that she attracted the second sexual act; because she had no boundaries since the first attack and she was looking for ways to feel validated and loved. Through feelings of low self-esteem and worthlessness Frances was always trying to control her world. This was her way of trying to feel safe.

On Frances' first day of school, when she was only 6 years of age, she was shamed by her teacher. Because she talked to someone in class next to her, she was placed in a corner as punishment. That was a painful day for her. She felt wronged, blamed and humiliated. Because of this Frances has always been afraid of anyone in authority. These beliefs and feelings perpetuated through her adult life. So the more shameful and guilty she felt, the more she judged herself, and the more she saw evidence around her that made her believe her life will never be different.

When Frances reached her dating years she always chose men who emotionally abused her. She realizes now that she did not respect and love herself nor did she feel attractive. Although she did not enjoy sex, she had a hard time saying no to people. Even if it meant that not saying "no" would cause her distress. She now realizes that the incident when she was three contributed in many ways to her difficulty of refusing people.

In the beginning of her marriage years, she had many challenges. She was confronted with her sexuality and her unresolved issues with men regarding the abuse. Her insecurities with herself caused many challenges with her daughter. Frances was trying to run her daughter's life and also trying to change her husband. Through her quest to heal herself, she has found ways to move beyond her pain and resolve her issues with men. And through this she realized that she could not change them, she can only change herself.

Frances chose a profession were she looked after sick people, just as her mother did. She became the ultimate caretaker. This job also made her feel like a victim and many times she felt like she was being bullied by those in authority over her. Frances now realizes, that besides allowing herself to be overpowered at the age of three and the other acts that followed, she continued to attract situations and events that showed her that she is a victim and that she cannot be in her own power.

Frances' insecurities caused her many stressful days at work. Frances' health deteriorated to the point that she considered quitting her full- time job. Her failing health brought her to a point in her life where she had to take notice, where she finally had to deal with her unresolved past. She was eventually forced to leave work. She feels now that she was looking for some way to kill herself. Some way to leave this painful existence she was living. Because she was such a caretaker, she had to find a way to justify to herself and to others why she can no longer take care of them.

Through this realization, Frances decided that she was no longer going to allow the events that happened so long ago to affect her future Due to this awareness and decision, her unhappy marriage improved beyond her wildest expectations, her relationship with her daughter blossomed. Her daughter surprised her by seeking help to improve her life. Frances went from working part-time in a job that was creating and adding to her home pressures to a situation where she now works out of her home in her holistic practice. She feels happier, good about herself and treats herself lovingly.

Many who have been either physically or emotionally abused in the past have feelings of unworthiness. “I am not worthy, I am not good enough, and I do not deserve to have healthy, happy, loving relationships” becomes their mantra. So in order for them to be happy, they have to be willing to free themselves through changing their perceptions, and eventually their beliefs. And they need to be willing to take ownership of their part in the creating. Now Frances understands fully that she chose these experiences. These agreements may have been made by her before she came into physical form. And if not, through her thoughts and feelings and fears she attracted all of it.

Even though Frances was using many of these processes to improve her life, nothing seemed to make her feel confident and sure of herself. Something was missing, until that day when she finally allowed herself to get to the bottom of why she has always felt a lack of self-worth. If we grew up in a home were we were constantly told that we were stupid, worthless and that we would never amount to anything; if we were brought up believing what our caretakers told us, we will start living our lives in accordance with what we perceived was the truth. Thus our thinking, feelings and beliefs will become our experience.

Our prisons are full of people who were raised that way. For over seven years I have volunteered at a penal institution along with some other practitioners. We assist the inmates to let go of their anger and frustration around their past relationships. Also to help them find ways to forgive themselves and those they have challenges with; and to help them understand why they are in these situations.

As long as they viewed themselves as being unworthy and not deserving, their futures would continue to produce what they had created up to this point in their lives.

Like all of us, we act out of our pain. These inmates are just products of their upbringing. The same applies to Frances. She did not feel good about herself, so she attracted events that proved to her she was not a worthwhile being. If we were not shown love, we will grow up not loving ourselves. And if I do not love me, how can I love you.

Tom Nesbitt's Story

Tom grew up in a home where both parents were alcoholics. The parents never demonstrated any love or affection to their son. As a result, Tom attracted many unhealthy relationships. His partners physically and emotionally abused him. They disappointed him, lied to him, kept him waiting, withheld money from him and many times withheld sex from him. Because of this treatment, Tom started to hate himself more and more. Before long, with many convictions to his name, he was heading down a road of disaster. Through all of this there was a part of Tom that loved to help people. This was the one thing in his life he loved to do. When he was doing this he felt worthwhile. He also loved when people praised him for his willingness to assist them.

Tom dreamed of having a better life. He spent hours by himself just dreaming of some possible great things happening to him. With a result he attracted someone who took a great interest in him. This person wanted him to do something with his life. This friend offered to help him with any studies he wanted to take. Tom decided to go to college and get some formal training in Human Resources.

Tom successfully completed his studies. He was among the top ten in the class. He now holds a successful well paying job.

By this friend showing an interest in Tom, making him feel worthy, it boosted his self-esteem and helped Tom to move forward and create more of what he wanted in his life.

Other ways these clients used to move forward were: they focused and talked more about what they wanted, used positive visualization as Tom did, and did a lot of appreciating as Irina did. For many of us, the negative beliefs are so large and hold so much resistant energy, that we find it difficult to just turn our attention off the problem. The challenge is to keep our feelings in a positive place and focused only on what we now want To find another feeling that feels a little better than the one you are experiencing now. Like the baby taking the first step, if they fail they try again until they feel more confident and more assured about themselves.

When I started to think about this book, I had some reservations about my ability to do this. Because of this thinking and my feelings of inadequacy, I attracted some frustrations along the way. What I asked the universe for initially was to have fun in the process of writing the book. I wanted it to be a fast, easy unfolding of my story and my teachings, and that the book would be successful. Most of all I wanted to have fun and enjoy the process. Even though I set these intentions in place my underlying feelings were insecure and my thoughts were I am not good enough to fulfill this task. These insecure feelings and thoughts manifested situations and events that did not make me feel good. During the period, I placed more of my thoughts on what I did not like about how the process of the book was unfolding.

Then I realized I was doing it again, which was "putting myself on hold." This was being mirrored back to me by what was happening around the book. When I took ownership for what I was creating. I did this by reminding myself of all my past accomplishments; I did not force myself to believe that I am definitely capable of producing this book, that all I had to do was reconnect to my higher self; remind myself of all the skills and tools I have to feel my own inner strength and to draw on that strength; and to trust that what I am now intending and asking for around my book is on its way to me.

What I knew was that as long as I stayed happy the universe knew what I wanted and by continuing to feel good, my prayer was heard.

In a matter of days of talking more about what I wanted about the unfolding of my book, I was feeling better. Ideas started to flow and I felt confident and ready to go again. Not long after I did this, doors started to open, insights came, ideas started to flow, people came forward passionate to help me in whichever way they could. As soon as I took myself off hold, by me feeling worthwhile, deserving and confident that I can write this book, my passion, joy, energy, excitement and most importantly my faith in myself returned. I was back on track and it felt so good to feel reconnected again.

Self-esteem And Self-worth Visualization

Find a comfortable place to lie or sit. Turn down the ringer on the telephone. Make sure the temperature in the room is exactly as you like it to be. Feel your body being fully supported as you lay. Inhale and exhale a few times and on the inhalation imagine the breath passing through your throat down through your chest, through the muscles in the stomach. Be conscious of relaxing all the layers of muscles in this area. Now continue to exhale while guiding the breath down through the hips, buttocks, the thighs and out through the legs and feet.

Now breathe in for the count of 4 and then exhale for the count of 4. Then continue to breathe in to the count of 5 and hold the breath for 5 and exhale for the count of 5, then breathe in for the count of 6. Hold the breath for the count of 7 and then exhale for the count of 7. Now taking one more long breath in, and on the exhalation if you have any further tension in the body that you are aware of, use this final exhalation to release this. Make sure your shoulders are relaxed and dropped. The muscles in your shoulder blade area are now fully relaxed, so are the arms and chest area. Down into the stomach, hips and large muscles in the hips and legs all the way down to your legs and out through your feet. You are now feeling very relaxed, but aware.

Now imagine yourself going through your day. Notice your recent thoughts and how you have been feeling. Have you been judging yourself or others? Are you having feelings of frustration around them, maybe wanting them to do things your way? Do you believe that your way is the right way and their way is the wrong? As you allow yourself to recall and observe these situations, notice your thoughts and feelings. Are your thoughts about these situations and people positive or negative? Notice how the body feels when you are interacting with these people in a negative way. And if the interaction is positive also notice how the body feels. Have you been feeling more pain and tension in your body lately? Listen to your words as you interact with these people who you have challenges with. Maybe it is your mother, father, sisters, brothers, employer, employee or mate. Notice how much energy it takes to get them to listen to you and do what you would like them to do. Observe yourself giving them advice, and how many times they have no intention of hearing your words. Notice how much this frustrates you because you feel that they are wrong and at fault.

Notice the tension in the body as you think and see your interacting with them. Also notice how they react as you try to give them advice and try to change them. You may be so busy trying to get your point across and so involved with trying to fix them that you do not observe how they may be feeling. You do not see their pain and anguish.

Now that you have allowed yourself to see their reactions to you, see yourself now being willing to allow them to be who they are. No need to try and change them. Feel your acceptance of them. As you are allowing others to be who they are, notice how your body starts to feel. Now that you are no longer worrying about them, feel how the body starts to respond to your thoughts. Your thoughts of acceptance, love and understanding will allow you to let go of the role of caretaker and adviser. Feel how the body is responding to your letting go of your resistance to their behaviour.

Now bring forth all the aspects of yourself, from all your past lifetimes Take in a few more deep breathes as you feel more and more connected to your source and who you truly are.

Now that you will not be spending so much time worrying about them, what would you be doing now with all this free time and energy you have? Allow yourself to imagine how you will be using all these minutes, hours and days on yourself to fulfill some of the dreams you have for yourself. Notice how the body responds as your start to allow these images to unfold and present themselves. Feel or imagine renewed energy streaming into the body. Notice how much lighter and free the body feels. Maybe the pain that you had before this exercise seems to have melted away.

You may tell yourself that you will no longer abandon you because you are important too. Your release does not mean you do not love them but that your need to love yourself first. When you are happy, you can help others be happy. You realize now that by being frustrated and angry with them you were judging them and this does not make them happy and does not help them. You now realize that this caretaking and trying to fix people (who may not want to change) has not brought you joy because your dreams and desires were placed on hold. If you have any guilty thoughts of abandoning them, know that they will be fine and that they will find their way in their own life journey.

Now imagine yourself standing in front of a mirror, or look into a mirror and tell yourself "How others choose to live their lives, is no longer my business. I stay focused on me. I am important. Look deep into your eyes and feel the power of your word. Feel the commitment you have just made to yourself. Breathe in and out slowly 3 times. You may also want to say some positive and encouraging affirmations to yourself, things that you like about yourself. Make sure you hold the eye contact by continuing to say words that you love and like about yourself.

After saying these positive empowering invocations you may notice that you are standing taller. There is a sparkle in your eyes. Notice how you are feeling from the inside out.

See yourself now walking through the day with so much energy. You have a new sense of purpose for who you now are out in the universe. This new you feels so good! Notice now how you interact with people, just letting them be who they are. Feel how your body responds, and how good it is to feel no judgment towards them. You may want to thank those people for teaching you this powerful lesson. You now realize that you do not need to be a caretaker to others and that you are to love yourself and live your dreams. Let go of any more tension and feel the excitement inside of you as you start to live your life in a more joyful, happy way.

See yourself getting on with new things in life like meeting new friends and being happy. It feels good to focus on your own happiness because those you used to worry about are getting on with their lives.

Notice how good the body is feeling. How the mind is now filled with all kinds of happy excited ideas and images. You cannot wait to write down or draw some of these images and information. You feel ready now to implement some of these new ideas. You feel a sense of peace yet you are so energized and very focused.

You may be at work at home, whatever it is you are doing. Notice how you are feeling as you move through this day interacting with different people. Notice how much more confident you are feeling and behaving. Notice how others respond to you now that your responses are coming from a more empowered secure place. They may give you compliments, ask if you cut your hair or changed your hairstyle. They recognize that there is something different about you. Just observe how they interact differently to you, and how you are now feeling inside about yourself.

See yourself in a social setting mingling and enjoying yourself and enjoying the people around you. Notice how easily you start a conversation and respond to others' interaction with you. Notice how good you feel to be there.

Now take this image and feelings to the future about 5 years from now. See yourself the same way. Very confident, clear and focused, living your life and fulfilling the dreams you set forth for yourself.

Now allow your mind to take you to some other pleasant situation where you are living your dreams.

Affirm To Yourself That If Ever You Feel Insecure Again You Will Bring Yourself Back To The Mirror And Remind Yourself Who You Truly Are.

Bring all those passionate feelings you have for yourself and your future back with you.

Exercises

1) Journal your experience.

2) You may want to draw the vision of the new self you saw.

3) You may want to write some empowering affirmations to yourself.

4) You may want to write any new ideas and goals that came to your mind.

5) Write a letter to those who you feel judged you; you do not have to mail the letters.

6) Write about your imaginary day. Be sure to include how you feel.

7) Write about when you imagined yourself 5 years from now.

8) Write about how others responded to the new you.

9) Draw how you saw yourself, full of confidence and feeling good and about your future dreams.

10) Prepare a list (as many pages as you can) of empowering words to yourself. It could be a sentence or it could be a letter you wrote to yourself.

Some Suggested Statements:

"I am worthy of having a healthy body."
"I am worthy of having a healthy, happy relationship."
"I am intelligent."

Look into your eyes and say these sentences or read this to yourself. Notice how you are feeling as you speak to yourself. You may want to record what you say so that you can play this back to yourself and notice how you sound. Do you sound connected to your words? Are you just saying these words or does it feel genuine?

After listening to yourself from the tape you may want to read the words and record what you say again and hear what you sound like the second time. You may find that the more you read the words to yourself you will feel and sound connected to what you are saying.

AFFIRM: WHAT IF TOMORROW I WERE TO FEEL WORTHY OF HAVING ALL MY DREAMS COME TRUE?

Student comments

"For me, it's been a tremendous help, especially in letting go of old habits and beliefs that have been stifling the joy in my life. I am constantly, daily, easily, using the techniques. It's all second nature now. Life gets better and better. I have manifested a fantastic co-creating mate, a dog, a horse, a dream house, vacations, money, four vehicles, love, ease, well-being, and I am not afraid to want more. Life is sweet, sexier, more brilliant, more generous. I've changed This work is empowering, liberating, and holistic. Hang on for the ride of your life. ENJOY! BLESSINGS AND BLISS" E.C.

"If you ask me for the successes, they are too numerous. I have had the dream vacations of many lifetimes. I have had the opportunity to travel around the world for free and have gone to Europe several times, South America and to the west coast and east coast of North America I have had dinners with Kings and diplomats and common folk as well. I have manifested a free car and money to pay for two others. I have received free money to buy a house. I have attracted two businesses and am now in the process of creating a third. I am in an allowing relationship. I love my dog, I love my mate, I love my job, I love my life. Thanks for the opportunity to write this. It has raised my energy tenfold and hope that it raises yours too in reading it." B.I.

Closing comments

When we decide to take our lives back, meaning to not continue living from our parents' or our peers' perceptions, feelings and emotions, we will start to feel better about ourselves. And when the self-critic emerges, this is our opportunity to decide if we want to continue the neuroses of others or to empower ourselves and make a decision based on what will please and empower us. Through this we will learn to follow our own guidance and to trust in our decisions. Also to not feel guilty when the outcome we were expecting is the one we wanted. It does not matter as this is our life and we get to choose. There is no right or wrong anyway, we just manifest in accordance to how we think and feel. Now we know that if things do not turn out the way we want it to, all we have to do is change how we have been thinking and feeling about what we have been asking for. This is our life and we get to choose. So take your life back and make decisions based on what makes you feel good.

Synopsis

For the next few days practice appreciation and focus upon whatever makes you feel good. Be who you want to be, not who others expect you to be. Be willing to think and speak and feel positive thoughts about yourself. Be selfish enough and only do what makes you feel good. Doing so does not mean you do not love them anymore. It is to change how you feel about yourself, and when you change how you feel about yourself you will attract the joy, health, success and prosperity that you want. You will start to see the evidence of these steps working for you.

You will start thriving and the universal powers will provide you what you want. Now that you have the confidence you are entitled to, create a goals list filled with specific things you want in your life, and enjoy the feeling that attracting them provides.

FEAR
ANXIETY

Chapter Four

Fear and Anxiety

Joyous Living Skill #4: Our fear is our higher self telling us that what we fear, we desire to change.

Many of us live in a place of fear every day of our lives. We fear the unknown, we fear failure, and we fear death. We fear not being good enough, we fear illness, we fear wellness, we fear abundance and we fear being alone. Our fear is a message from our higher self. When fear or anxiety appears; this is our higher self telling us that whatever we fear right now is not in harmony with what we are wanting for ourselves with regard to our dreams and desires. Fear is your emotional guidance trying to get your attention, alerting you that this negative emotion is not serving you. The specific area where fear resides is the precise area we want to change in our lives. If we fear commitment, we desire a happy, healthy long-term relationship. If we fear our success, that is exactly what we desire. Fearing failure is the paradox in the equation - we don't fear failure, we fear success, because that's what we want. This principle applies to every area of our lives. Fearing fear itself sucks the energy out of us leaving anxiety, depression, resentment, shame and guilt in its wake. We cannot be happy thinking fearful thoughts.

When clients come to me complaining about depression and/or anxiety, these emotions were picked up from their parents. When I ask them "Who in the family is anxious and fearful?" We discover that one or sometimes both parents were very anxious and fearful. Living in the same home the child had no way of escaping, so many children assumed their parents emotions. These feelings that the children have taken on may be hidden for years. Then as they become adults and encounter their own challenges and pressures, these feelings will start to surface. Sometimes these feelings express themselves in other behaviours, such as anger, depression, and aggression. Once my client recognizes this process, he can decide to let go of the cloud that has shadowed him for all these years.

For instance, one of my client's fathers was very driven to excel. He worked hard and long hours. Because of the father's behaviour resulting in his high achievement, the child grows up observing and feeling the father's need to be the best. The father then starts to place the same standards on the child. So no matter how well the child does in school, it never satisfies his father. The grades are never high enough. If the child does not do well, the child knows some form of punishment will reprimand him. It could mean the strap or privileges being taken away from him.

Most likely, this father grew up under similar pressure. His parents applied the same kind of pressure on him to succeed. Perhaps his family lived in poverty, or conversely, lived in luxury, but the result was the same. If he endured a disadvantaged childhood, the pressure to escape the poverty was intense. If his background was enriched, there was pressure to maintain or increase his standard of living as an adult. There was never a message that he was good enough as he is, and that his essential self rather than the economics of his family should dictate his choices. Even though others may praise and admire him for his accomplishments, he always feels anxious and feels he must try harder on the treadmill of his life. This person lives his life in anguish. He will never allow himself to enjoy his accomplishments. He will always be pressing forward for more. It is important to point out that there is nothing wrong with striving for the best and to be successful as long as we enjoy the journey.

This is not a judgment on our parents. They taught us what they learned from their parents. Parental messages include: this is a bad world, we have to be careful, do not speak to strangers, this world is not safe; the world is in a bad way. It was always someone else's fault as to why things were not the way they wanted.

Barbara, one of my clients, expresses it this way. "Fear seems to be a constant in my life. From the moment I was born, fear seems to have been my only state of being. I could always depend on the foreboding cloud to be present in my daily life. It wasn't until my studies with Marlene that I began to understand and alter the source of my fear, replacing it with joy in my everyday life."

The other manifestation of fear in my clients' lives is denial. Some of them are so out of touch with their feelings, they are operating on automatic pilot and wonder why there life is not working out they way the deserve. As another client told me, "I do not remember being fearful. I was so out of touch with my feelings. I felt nothing. There was no room for my feelings. I was so caught up with the emotions of everyone else in the family especially my parents. I was the surrogate husband for my mother and the surrogate wife for my father. Marlene's teachings helped me to face my feelings, then move past them to heal my relationships with my parents and finally around my marriage." S.C.

People make choices based on their fear. At different points in my life, my choice to escape fear has led me to make choices. This has resulted in some good and some not so very good choices. As soon as I claimed to own this emotion myself, my healing began. It is always easier to blame another for our burdens, but it does not lift the burden from our shoulders, nor does it lighten our load. Only through facing the fear, can we alleviate it. Believing in the power of the present, we can face our fear and alter our feelings toward our future.

Everything I learned from the teachings I discussed in Chapter One, I incorporate into my work with my clients. Some may initially need more hands-on healing work, but I tell all my clients that although this is helpful it is just a temporary fix, a Band-Aid solution. The reality is their thinking and how they are feeling about their challenges in their life that will affect how they feel. They need to address their thoughts, beliefs and how they are feeling about themselves. When they understand how they attracted the events and situations into their lives that are not pleasing them, by learning new skills and new ways of thinking and feeling, they can empower themselves to live their better lives.

Some who come to me for help have read many spiritual books and have been exposed to this work. Because they already understand how their thoughts produce their lives, they may need to be refocused on their own healing process. Others have the knowledge, but not the skills to actualize the lives they say they want. The majority of my clients accept the work, but need support in completing it. Depending on their situation, there are many avenues to the same end.

Mary's Story

Mary grew up in a home where there was a lot of negativity, where both her parents were anxious and fearful. Mary and her parents lived through a war where many days they had no food. They lived in constant fear of the circumstances surrounding them. Even though Mary was in her fifties when I first met her, she still lived her life constantly worrying about the possible shortage of food. She spent a lot of their family income on keeping her cupboards stocked, buying dozens of the same products fearing the possibility that she may run short.

She never went anywhere without food in her car. Sometimes the impulse was so strong that even though she was invited to dinner or for a weekend where all the meals were provided, she took her own food. Once Mary realized how this fear was controlling her, she decided she no longer wanted to live this way. In a very short period of time, after applying some of the exercises expressed in this book, she was able to live a happy life.

The clients are encouraged to complete four sessions and during these four sessions they are helped to see clearly how their thoughts, feelings, beliefs, perceptions and where they have placed their focus, has kept them stuck. The severity of the challenge that they have does not matter, the skills that are imparted to them are in many ways the same with a few changes depending on the individual.

Everyone is treated individually. Someone who has been sexually abused or someone with a so-called normal background will be helped to understand how they have been attracting the events and situations into their lives that are now challenging them. So regardless of the challenge, the first thing they need to understand is how they have been thinking and feeling. Once they understand this, and they are strongly motivated to change, miracles happen.

For instance, someone who has an incest challenge may be more committed to move forward and heal than another whose story is of a more normal background. The strong desire and the decision to now move forward is what will outweigh the enormity of the situation.

There are those who have been sexually abused and move past their concerns relatively quickly and then there are those who may have a lesser challenge but may be more sensitive and fearful with the result they have more resistance to healing.

Once they clearly see the series of events that brought their situation to be manifested, many of them then decide to change.

In many of these cases low self-esteem and rejection is apparent. So I generally suggest they write pages and pages of things that they appreciate and like about themselves. I also suggest that they write pages of things about the people in their lives that they have challenges with.

Trust and guilt play a major role in many of these lives. Those who have guilt fear being discovered, while the others have fear in trusting anyone. Once they understand where their issues started and how it will continue if they don't change, many are then strongly motivated to change. In many case it does not take long for them to see the evidence in their lives and they start to feel happier and lighter.

In the first session as homework/fun work, they are asked to make a list of the things that they now would like to have in their lives.

Once they have completed the list they write a pretend letter to a friend including all these wonderful things they now want in their lives. They either e-mail this list to me, or bring them to the next session so that we can now expand on the dream and help them align their feelings to what they want.

They are also asked to make a list of the things about themselves that they like and appreciate. And if there are people in their lives that they are having challenges with they are asked to make a list of the things they can appreciate about the person even if it is only one thing.

Then they are asked to make an itemized list about things in general that they can appreciate.

This is done because if they focus on appreciating themselves, others and anything else they like, this will make them feel good. And when they feel good there is no room for fear or anxiety. They are not a magnet for attracting any unpleasant situations!

In the following sessions we will continue to work toward the goals that they have set for themselves. They are now in touch with how they are feeling about their fears.

One simple step that is suggested, and which has helped many, is for them to take some nice deep breaths when the fear and anxiety strikes.

Another simple exercise that is encouraged is to have them focus on their feet when they feel anxious and fearful. This is a Therapeutic Touch exercise, where you focus your attention on your feet and imagine that you are growing roots on the balls and soles of your feet. See nice strong roots and imagine them going deep down into the ground. Send them all the way down. Notice if they are an even thickness. If not, bring them into balance with each other. Now send the fear and anxiety all the way down into the bowels of the earth. Take in a few nice deep long breaths and exhale all the way down through your legs and feet.

There are times though that I may feel guided to encourage some of them to do some form of transformational emotional work because I sense deep anger, judgment of self or others and/or guilt. This may include a combination of treatments, breath work, counseling and my two-day workshop "Learning To Move

Forward." This powerful workshop shows them clearly why they are unhappy with what is happening in their lives, based on how they have been thinking, feeling and therefore attracting the situations and events into their lives that are not pleasing them. On the second day they are provided with different skills to use in their daily lives to create for themselves the life they want.

What happens in a session all depends on the person's desire to move forward. Some come frothing at the mouth, they are tired of where their lives have taken them and now they are ready to commit to themselves and heal, and then there are those who want to test the process. So I treat them all individually.

The sessions could include treatments such as Therapeutic Touch, Reiki, CranioSacral Therapy and counseling, or they may combine treatment, discussions and some Transformational Workshops. The treatments help them relax and feel less anxious and can reduce pain. The Transformational work gives them an opportunity to choose to release the beliefs and fears they have been holding regarding the past or present events. Many come to workshops, many come for individual sessions, and many have consultations over the phone.

Some times if I feel that the person is resisting and controlling, I will suggest an exercise called The Wall. It is a bioenergetic exercise that is done up against the wall. It builds up energy in the person's body resulting in them having to let go and get out of their minds. This enables them to feel more. Many have profound experiences and in many cases they will remember instances that they have blocked. Most of the time, these memories help the person move forward. This exercise can be painful on the legs, but there are many who still believe that through pain comes gain. Many times through this one last blastoff struggle, they finally allow themselves to move forward.

Ultimately, this is the client's process, I recommend and advise that there are easier ways to heal but it is their choice to select the process they want to explore with me to bring them to their goals.

Barbara's Story

"One of my attempts to escape fear caused me to marry a person that I did not know. Although, I now know I should have dealt with the "fear" before making any major life choices. Our son was born two years into our marriage. He is a wonderful young man. We were a family until I finally had the courage to leave. For eight years we moved back and forth from Europe to Canada. My husband could not commit to work; his experience of a marriage was the opposite of mine.

Not that my experience was better than his. His father was not a "present father," his mother worked many hours to support two children, leaving the eldest to care for the youngest. Sometimes sending the eldest away to family to be looked after (where he experienced different forms of emotional and sexual abuse). At this point in my writing, I can see similarities, mirrors if you will, in my ex-husband's life and my life as children.

My parents emigrated from Europe in 1966. They worked hard, bought their first home after four years in Canada. My dad worked two jobs, and my mom worked full-time. And I was left at home to be cared for by the landlord of the flat we lived in, or by my parents calling home during their breaks to see that I was okay, or to tell me that it was time to go to school I grew up alone, until my sister arrived. Then I was responsible for her. My sister and I now would be left at the baby-sitter's to be cared for. Neither parent was present in our lives. My sister was eventually sent to our grandparents in Europe to be cared for." B.R.

Barbara's story illustrates the damage caused by parental neglect, even though her parents felt they were doing the best they could for their children by working hard. And perhaps they had no choice in order to survive. However, from Barbara's perspective she was not important enough to her parents for them to be present in her life. The first thing she needed to understand was she chose this situation, these parents, these siblings to learn some lessons before she was born into this plane. Her circumstances were not her fault, nor her parents. Rather they were challenges designed to increase her understanding of how the world works and how through self-examination she could have the life she wants. The first step is knowing what you don't want in life. Once that is determined you shift your focus to what you do want. Fear takes up so much time and energy that my clients don't see another way of feeling until they are exposed to these teachings. Using the skills for joyous living, my clients understand their fear, then learn to eliminate it through acceptance and appreciation for themselves and the sources of their fear. During our initial four private sessions she was made aware of her thoughts, feelings, beliefs and perceptions regarding these fears.

1) How her parents' neglect caused many of her fears.

2) During the "Learning to Move Forward" workshop, she saw clearly how her thoughts and feelings were the cause of her fears and anxieties.

3) She saw the power of the “Learning to Move Forward” workshop and repeated it a couple times every time she aligned herself closer and closer to her desires. She saw powerful evidence of how much happier she was.

4) She also did Breath Work, hands-on healing sessions, telephone consultations and attended some Healing Circles. She was strongly motivated to make changes in her life. And it showed.

5) She was given skills in all of these sessions, which consisted of writing pages and pages of appreciative things about herself, her parents and anything else in her life she could appreciate.

6) She incorporated The Invocation found in Chapter Six, Health.

7) She wrote a pretend letter to a friend telling this friend what a great life she was now living, and how what she dreamed about was now coming to fruition.

8) Most importantly, she was aware of how she was feeling. She never condemned herself for feeing depressed or fearful. She just reached for a feeling that would make her feel a little better.

9) She is now able to bring herself to a better feeling place because she has many skills to do this now.

Another fear common to many of my clients is the fear of being discovered. For instance, they were in jobs where they did not feel capable and confident, even though their peers held them in high regard and their employers hired them because of their superior credentials. Throughout their professional lives, these people feel insecure, anxious and afraid. They feel like actors in roles, which are way over their heads even though there is, plenty of applause after every performance. When they return to the privacy of their dressing room, they remove their costumes and look in the mirror to see the fear on their face.

Jim's Story

Jim, on the other hand, lived in a home where he observed two distinct parental practices. His mother appeared to him to be very positive while his father was very negative. His mother always praised and encouraged him, whereas the father called him all kinds of demeaning names. This confused Jim, with the result his grades suffered in school. In many ways Jim understood the work, but there was always a part of him that felt insecure, not good enough. He also felt that he had to try harder and even though many saw him as capable and doing good work, he felt like he was fooling the world. He did not feel inside the same positive way others viewed him. He had many moments of great overwhelming fear, which lead to panic attacks.

When Jim finally completed his studies and went to work, he was also viewed as very capable (which he was). Oftentimes, Jim's fear and anxiety became so overwhelming for him, because he was afraid others would discover his secret. This fear of being discovered added to his stress, so he decided to leave his job.

Jim then made the decision that he needed to heal this situation so that he could live a life of happiness and peace. Once he understood the source of his anxiety, where this all started for him, then by applying some of the following skills, Jim was able to change how he felt about himself.

Visualization

Find a comfortable place to lie down. This is your time to relax and to create and enjoy your time with yourself. Dim the lights. You may want to play some soothing music. Do whatever you need to do for yourself to feel comfortable.

Some people imagine the angels surrounding them; some surround themselves with the white light. Take a few breaths in and out. With each inhalation breathe in a feeling of peace and on the exhalation breathe out any fear, anxieties, concerns and emotional or physical pain. Feel the body softening and relaxing more and more. You are feeling very peaceful and quiet and relaxed.

Now take yourself back in time. Remember all the pleasant things and happy experiences that have happened in your life. Recall those times. Bring all your senses into the meditation. If you see yourself on the beach recalling a past vacation, feel the sand on your feet, smell the sea air, and feel the sun and ocean breeze on your face. Your body feels great and you feel very alive and energized. Who else is there with you? If there are others with you, what are they saying or doing? Bring only happy people into your visualization.

Maybe you are visualizing yourself walking your dog. See him or her running happily ahead of you. What are you seeing as you walk? Smell the fresh morning or evening air.

See yourself moving confidently through your day. What interesting creative things are you doing? How are others interacting and responding to your happy, calm, secure approach? What important task are you involved in? Notice the ease in which you approach an assignment. Maybe it is a presentation you need to prepare, or a task you have never done before. Remind yourself of all your great skills and past achievements. You love being at your workplace.

You may see yourself with your friends and/or family, having a great time with each other. This is your time to create and imagine whatever you want. Take as much time as you need to be in this fantasy. If you fall asleep, that is fine also. This is your time to nurture yourself. When you are ready, feel the support under you, open your eyes.

Exercises

1) Write pages and pages of how you appreciate yourself and what you like about yourself.

2) Now take that list and read it into a tape. Do this 3 times.

You will notice that the more you say the words to yourself the more believable they will sound and feel.

3) Read this to yourself while standing in front of a mirror. Look into your eyes as you read this list or as you listen to your voice on the tape Breathe in and out after every sentence. Feel the impact of your encouraging words.

4) Carry the list with you or on cards so when you get that sinking feeling, "I am not good enough," reach for the list and read it to yourself. Before long you will be feeling better.

5) Imagine you are someone you admire, Oprah, for instance. When you feel insecure say to yourself "What would Oprah say or do now?"

6) Make "I am" statements, such as: "I am intelligent, I am creative; I am a good responsible conscientious worker."

7) Make a list of people and things in your life that you appreciate.

8) Carry the list with you and/or tape them so when you feel challenged, reading these lists or listening to the tape will help you

feel better and more connected to your source. Reading the list or listening to the tape will help you feel less fearful and anxious.

Student Comment

"Thanks to Marlene, I finally found the courage to leave a family business in which I was unhappy for a long time. I went to further my education. I appreciate all that my parents have done for me. My future plan is to move away from my parents, buy a home for my son and I. Now that I understand where my fears started, these teachings have helped me to free myself, feel more confident, I trust my decisions and I am also loving myself more. I now realize I gave these fears power by my constant attention to them and to the thoughts I did not want in my life, and that my negative feelings about my past only made me feel worse. I now know that these negative thoughts and feelings were not compatible to what I desired. This is what perpetuated my fears and anxieties." B.V.

Synopsis

When we understand what fear is and where the fear is coming from, we can move toward overcoming these emotions. By placing the facts in the proper perspective and understanding where these fearful beliefs started, we can start to live the joyful lives we were intended to have. Fear is our guide to let us know that what we are now thinking, focusing on or feeling is not in harmony to what we desire. Later in this book, you will learn the importance of placing your thoughts on the things you do want in your life, rather than allowing the things you don't want to distract you on your journey.

chapter Five

Relationships

JOYOUS LIVING SKILL # 5: RIGHT NOW YOU HAVE THE POWER TO CREATE A BETTER RELATIONSHIP. GET HAPPY, AND YOU WILL HAVE A HAPPY RELATIONSHIP.

In keeping with our theme of living today, our discussions of relationships illustrate the power point of living in the present. The importance of the present is easy to understand in the other chapters which deal with Self-Esteem, Health, Higher Self, Fear and Forgiveness, all subjects which occur in the Now. However, whenever we introduce another person into the Now we tend to shift our focus to the past if it's a long-term relationship, or the future if you are in the first blush of a relationship. Rarely, if ever, do we consider the Now when trying to improve our relationships with our parents, our significant others, our work associates or our children. And that is the problem. As with every issue in our life, the solution lies in the power of the present.

When we discuss relationships the starting point is our relationship with self. When our relationships fall apart, it's not about our counterpart. Look in the mirror; it's about the face looking back at you. From a young age, we were taught that we were not to accept blame. Rather it is always someone else's fault. As children we blamed our friends, our teachers or our parents for our troubles. As adults, we still blame the government, our employers, teachers and parents for our sorrows.

Before we came into physical form, we chose our parents, our choices and our challenges. We learned to personalize everything in our environment. Ironically, that does not include accountability for our actions and the events which occur in our lives. We tend to accept our accomplishments, but deny our responsibilities, especially to ourselves. The human condition is to focus on our own individual world, when in fact we are creative beings, eager to co-create with each other. Part of that co-creation is to learn our lessons from the people who come into our lives. Our relationships are people who are generous enough to mirror the challenges we need to grow and progress down our chosen path. And we reciprocate by mirroring to them the lessons they need to progress on their chosen path.

When we are confronted with conflict, it is our choice to face this challenge. Our friends, families or associates are all reflections of who we are at this point in time. Their issues mirror ours. We need to take responsibility for anything that occurs in a relationship, confident that the conflict forces us to face our issues and rectify them. As long as I do not love me, I will attract events that will show me that I am unworthy and undeserving of good things in my life. Feeling like a victim, I will attract persecutors who will confirm that I am a victim. If I judge myself, others will judge me. Praising myself will attract praise from others.

Many people feel it is easier to simply leave a difficult relationship, and move on to another better one. Rather than improve their relationships, these people find others who will reinforce their self- image. We all know people who have married the same spouse over and over again. The names may change, but the challenges remain. Until they change their feelings about the challenges, the challenges will not change

For a moment reflect on a positive relationship you have or have had in your life. Feel the warmth in your chest when thinking about the person, experience the smile that softens your features while picturing that person in your mind's eye. Now, picture a person with whom you are in conflict, feel your face freeze, your body tense as that person inspires negative feelings in your body. As soon as you can replace that negativity with the warmth of positive or at the very least neutral feelings, all of your relationships will be happy and healthy.

Many clients come to me wanting to change the other person. "If he or she would only do this and stop doing that" then the relationship would work. As soon as my clients understand the only person they can change is themselves, and by doing so the others in their lives will either change in the positive or may leave in anger if they do not want to change, or possibly gracefully remove themselves from the relationship. This not only applies to the significant relationships in our lives, but to the casual ones as well.

Have you ever called someone, but in your heart you really would rather not have to make the call. These calls do not go well because you have called out of guilt or obligation. You cannot interact with this person unless they are feeling some form of reluctance about something in their life also. We reflect back to other situations and attract to ourselves in accordance with how we are thinking and feeling. It is no surprise that the outcome of the conversation may not be a pleasant one! It is important to think about what we bring to each of our encounters with others. Once we have discovered how we come on to others and how we interact each time, then we will be able to resolve and prevent much conflict.

As soon as you are willing to commit to doing this work, a miracle occurs and your relationships change. According to Buddha, there are many different paths to enlightenment, but enlightenment remains the same. Using our emotions as our guide, we may feel our way to long-lasting and joyous relationships. By monitoring your feelings, you will attract loving relationships into your life. You will move forward by moving past old patterns, beliefs and perceptions. Again, those around you do not have to change in order for you to get what you want. You can better the outcomes of your interactions with others by changing your responses, old habits and attitudes. No matter how desperate and gloomy the relationships look now, they can be transformed in a very short time when you apply the skills of joyous living.

Exercises

1) WRITE PAGES AND PAGES OF POSITIVE AND APPRECIATIVE THINGS YOU LIKE ABOUT YOURSELF.

2) WRITE PAGES AND PAGES OF POSITIVE AND APPRECIATIVE THINGS ABOUT PEOPLE IN YOUR LIFE YOU HAVE CHALLENGES WITH.

3) DO NOT JUST TALK ABOUT HOW MUCH YOU LOVE THEM; SHOW THEM THROUGH YOUR ACTIONS.

    a) Remember the time when things went well, when you met and were happy. Appreciate, appreciate and appreciate.

    b) Visualize the kind of relationship you want to have. Get happy even though the relationship is not the way you would like it to be. Without happiness, it will never be the way you desire.

c) Ignore the negative and appreciate the positive. Love them unconditionally. Do this for 30 days and watch the universe give you what you want in this relationship or a new and better one will come along.

d) When you are in an appreciative place you cannot be angry with these people who challenge you. You will remember who you truly are, the lover within.

Relationships with Our Birth Family

Before we arrived in this incarnation, we had all the knowledge we needed to create joyful and loving relationships. We accumulated these skills from our former lives. We knew that our emotional and spiritual selves would guide us to healthy relationships. Feeling happy meant the relationship was a good one, feeling sad meant we had to understand within ourselves what wasn't working and why. Soon after birth we looked forward to interacting with others and to living a happy life. At this point, our parents present our first challenge. Our physical survival depended on interaction with our parents. That is the first step we took to seek happiness outside of ourselves. To the degree our parents understood their roles as lovers and supporters, our early years are conflict free. Experts concur, parents cannot "spoil" infants. Infants communicate their discomfort, parents solve the problem, and there is no conflict. Infants remain true to themselves, and soon learn that a happy baby creates happy parents. This "honeymoon" period is short, for it is important that the baby begin to learn the lessons he intended prior to arriving on this planet. It is at this point conflict enters his paradise when he no longer meets his parents' expectations, or his parents want to spare him from some of the pain they have suffered, or in the worst case the parents pass their pain on to him in emotional or spiritual abuse or neglect. The baby's survival depends on his parents, so his coping skills separate him from his essential self. The more difficult the childhood is, the wider the separation from self.

In addition, children take in much of their parents' thoughts, attitudes, emotions and fears. As adults, many of our beliefs, perceptions, and feelings are manifestations of our parents' projections. Our first challenge is to recognize which beliefs are ours and which belong to our primary caregivers. Once we are aware, we can choose to no longer live our lives through their perceptions. We can reclaim our essential selves and start trusting our own emotional guidance system.

In order to make that change, we must stop our resentments, including blaming, hating, and regretting.

Parents are easy scapegoats for whatever goes wrong in our lives. Many parents abused, neglected and tormented their children when they acted out their own pain. Other parents took too much care of their children, not allowing them to learn from their mistakes, even trying to prevent mistakes before they happened. This, too, is a form of abuse and a challenge to the adult when he discovers the world is not as interested in saving him from himself as his parents were. And there are the parents who try to build themselves up by belittling or re-doing any effort their child makes. Even the good parents present challenges to their children during their lifetimes. It is important to realize that we contracted this relationship to learn our own lessons. When we can replace the resentment with the gratitude the relationship deserves, we will be well on our way to a healthy relationship with them.

Isaac's Story

Isaac could move on in his life once he came to terms with his past. Isaac's mother suffered from depression and could not handle the pressures of parenting. She created intense anxiety and fear in Isaac, because when he did not obey her or follow her instructions, she would leave the house for several hours. As he grew up, Isaac suffered from anxiety and panic attacks. He married a woman who was manic-depressive like his mother. Finally, he realized he needed to get help in order to work through his fears and unhappiness. Through counseling, Isaac began to recall his mother's difficulty controlling his crying, and how she would put on her coat and walk out the door. Isaac discovered that his own grandmother had used the same types of threats when his mother was a child. As he began to let go of his pain through compassion, Isaac began to realize why he was suffering from anxiety and how he had attracted a woman similar to his mother into his adult life. He began to understand why his mother had abused him and through forgiveness, Isaac turned his life around. He delved into his music career further and remarried. His second wife is a talented singer and appreciates his talents as well. Although he continues to suffer from occasional bouts of anxiety, he is able to work through his emotions by recognizing the source. Because Isaac had a strong desire to heal, he was able to meet many teachers, guides and friends along the way who enable him to speed up the process of healing and to get on with his life.

When clients come to me complaining about depression and/or anxiety, my initial response is "Who in the family is anxious and fearful?" Through our discussions it becomes clear to the client that these emotions were picked up along their way mostly from their parents. We discover that one or sometimes both parents were very anxious and fearful. As a child living in the same home with no way of escaping this behaviour, some children take on their emotions. These feelings that the children take on may be hidden for years. Then as they become adults and encounter their own challenges and pressures, these feelings will start to surface. Sometimes these feelings express themselves in other behaviour, such as anger. Once this is established the client can decide to let go of this behaviour that has haunted and held him back for all these years.

Our siblings are our contracts, too. We choose them as they chose us. Birth order makes a difference in behaviour development and personality. Older siblings bear the brunt of greater responsibility, while middle children will feel abandoned and ignored once a younger baby is born. So siblings also affect our behaviour. Parents compare children with each other. Parents will recognize the talents of one child and ignore the others. In addition to creating jealousy and friction, it fosters low self-esteem in all of the children. The favored child often feels guilty to be considered so special. As we emerge from the relative simplicity of infancy, our challenges increase as we expand our relationships in the world. And this is how it should be in order for us to learn.

Lena's Story

Forty-six-year-old Lena realized that her perceptions of her childhood had created much of her difficulties. After much counseling and soul searching, Lena now realizes that her birth father loved her. Because of her father's enthusiastic appreciation of her older sister's aptitude for sports, she did not believe he had enough love in his heart for her. As a result, Lena felt ignored by her parents, so she manifested anorexia in order to obtain attention. Consequently, her sisters bullied her which estranged her further, so she left home. She then began working on her anorexia. Lena understood why she had created her illness in order to get attention. She realized the importance of moving forward in order to relieve the pain of loneliness. She began her journey into healing through workshops, counseling and then assisting others. Lena understood that her inability to connect with her father and sisters created her illness for attention. Rather than perpetuate her pain, she forgave her father and siblings and was able to create healthy and happy relationships with each of them.

Natasha's Story

As an adult she now realizes that her mother was not there for her emotionally. This insight came to her in a Breath workshop. She is also now aware that she is not emotionally available with her relationships with men. She would create distance with them and she never made them feel that she was one hundred percent present for them. This was what her mother also did in her relationship with her husband, Natasha's father. As a result, Natasha ended two marriages and is now in her third significant relationship.

As a child she felt a lot of warmth and generosity. Because of her unique bond with her father she has always felt more comfortable with men in general. Natasha never trusted women and was always very competitive around them. Much of this behaviour she observed from her mother. Natasha's mother also did not have a healthy relationship with her mother. Through the work she has done on herself and the realizations she has made, she now feels just as comfortable with all her female friends and acquaintances.

Natasha is the oldest daughter and she always felt pressured to do well. This became a benefit because she had to support herself. Still, in spite of her independence she did not appreciate herself. Many of these insecurities and patterns she observed in her mother as a child. Her mother allowed people to take advantage of her. She did not love herself and that is why she withheld her love from her husband, Natasha's father.

As a child, Natasha was never told by her parents that she was loved. As a result, even though both her ex-husbands told her that they loved her, she did not trust or know what those words truly meant.

When her second relationship ended she worked on releasing her anger around the marriage. Also, she used many of the Invocations (See Chapter Seven on Health) daily; this brought her to the place of forgiveness for herself and her husband. She also took ownership for her part in the relationship. She understood clearly that she played a part in creating this experience, that there was no one to blame and it was best to move forward. She released him to love and light.

When we decide to recognize the pain of our upbringing, it is the first step to healing. When we take that first step we are on the road to happiness. The desire for change is foremost, and the time to change is Now! Our parents had their own pain from their own childhood, much of that they passed on to their children. This created a vicious pattern throughout many generations. We now have the knowledge to stop the cycle by having the courage to change our behaviour which will spare our children from the pain accumulated over the generations. Our family members came with their lessons to learn, too. And we have our part in their lessons as they have their part in ours. Understand it is no longer about someone being right and therefore the other is wrong. Rather it's a balance of teaching and learning on both parts. If we accept, understand and practice this concept, our future will have the happiness we deserve.

Karen's Story

Karen was abused as a child. Her mother locked her in a dark and damp closet for hours as a means of punishment or torture. She constantly ridiculed Karen and told her she was ugly. Her father was passive and provided no support or rescue to the suffering young girl. As a result, Karen grew up with very low self-esteem and a weight problem. She tried desperately to gain her mother's approval but to no avail. Karen dreaded visiting her parents once they were older because of ongoing conflict and fear. Because her father had not protected Karen, she grew up mistrusting men and attracted an abusive first marriage. Due to this, Karen became obsessively controlling in all of her relationships. In time, Karen realized she needed to overcome her feelings of sadness, shame and low self-esteem.

Through her work, Karen began to realize that she needed to lay down the blame and anger she was experiencing. Due to all the pain she had suffered, Karen was able to channel her experiences into producing and directing plays part-time. She was able to draw intense emotion from her actors because of her own experiences. She chose to turn her life around by creating workshops using art and music in order to help people release their anger and to work through their own emotional turmoil. Her childhood experiences had led her to her life's work and purpose. Along with this realization, Karen needed to accept that her mother would never provide her with an apology, recognition or unconditional love. Once Karen released her mother from blame and judgment, she was able to visit her parents with less fear and expectation. This realization helped Karen to move forward and to feel greater happiness. She attracted a happier marriage and later brought two daughters and a son into this world.

You can live your life repeating the same behaviour over and over again and getting the same results. Nothing will change in your life until you change your feelings and thoughts. Some of my clients needed to go back and revisit their past issues several times. By looking back at their past, these clients were able to recognize how their beliefs and attitudes had shaped their adult lives. They made the choice to move forward and to free themselves in a very powerful way by accepting the responsibility for their thoughts and feelings. Once they became accountable, they were able to eliminate blame and guilt in their lives. Those who underwent this process soon found themselves more peaceful, loving and appreciative.

Synopsis

Recognize the beliefs and perceptions you have which do not apply to you as an adult, because you received them from your parents. Exercise your Point of Power, by committing to changing now This is not a betrayal of your parents, because they, too, had their own lessons to learn as well as lessons to teach. Their attitudes no longer apply to your life. There are some cases where the best road to happiness is to distance yourself from your parents, and this too, is a lesson to learn and a lesson to teach.

Exercises

1) Recognize that your parents did their best they with the skills they had.

2) Be willing to take them out of the box, to see them differently.

3) Understand they have their pain and their story.

4) Be willing to forgive yourself and them. (See Chapter Six on Forgiveness.)

5) Understand that you made this agreement to have this experience or manifest these thoughts, feelings and actions.

How Do We Now Relate To Our Parents As Adults?

We tend to forget that, just as we came here all knowing, so did our parents. Just as we create our story during our time here in the physical, so did our parents. Many of the elderly will not change themselves, but they chose this and are entitled to live it. As adults we have a responsibility to ourselves to choose the relationship we want with them, too. Our parents will always see us as their children, perhaps not as adults. This, too, is part of the process. The degree to which we subscribe to this perception depends upon our adult beliefs. Do we feel like children in spite of our age? If so, why? Again, our responsibility is to analyze our feelings for our part in the relationship. If those feelings are negative, we can do what we need to do to change them and therefore improving the quality of the relationship.

Bob's Story

Because they were very negative and critical, Bob experienced many challenges with his parents. Both of them suffered from low self-esteem. They did not accept that their negativity had caused a great deal of anxiety and failure in Bob's life. Bob became determined to change his life and sought out counseling. Through this process he discovered that he had been contributing to the challenge because when his parents acted negatively towards him, he responded the same way. Nothing changed and he realized that the best time to work on this relationship would be when he was separated from and not interacting with his parents. Bob began to transform his feelings of bitterness into appreciation through a series of self-help workshops. He realized that a continued negative experience with his parents would perpetuate his own loneliness and unhappiness. He focused on anything positive that he could appreciate about his parents. Just with his shift in focus, Bob became more lighthearted and positive. They still have challenges in their relationships, but things have improved and the house is a happier place.

If one person in the family heals, this forces a shift in the dynamics among the others. We need to repair our relationships with our parents in order to move forward. We can have a loving relationship with our parents by following these strategies:

Exercises

1) We can acknowledge them for who they are. They did their best with what they knew.

2) Appreciate them for what they have done for us. Focus on one good thing they contributed in our lives.

3) We come here with all our knowledge from our other lives. They too have wisdom they can draw on and when we praise them, this will make them feel good. We help them to remember who they truly are.

4) Have patience with them.

Synopsis

We have choice, we get to choose. So we can choose to have loving relationships with our parents. Free them from all the hurts we feel they caused us; be willing to own our part in the manifestation. Love them no matter what we do not like about their behaviour. Know we are only getting what we are giving. Our experience with them is only a result of our thoughts, attitudes and beliefs about our relationship with them. We all act from our pain and so do our parents. They did the best they could with the skills and tools they had.

Our own children

More than ever before, parenting today presents a challenge. There is a great emphasis on child psychology, dealing with childhood defiance and the outside dangers of violence. We often delve into a series of "How to parenting" gimmicks in order to minimize the mistakes that some of us may have experienced from our parents. Despite our best efforts, we turn to the parenting methods our parents used. We take on their fears and beliefs on an unconscious level. Many clients, who complain of depression and/or anxiety, will find that the root of their pain stems from childhood. This is not to blame our pain on our parents. Children sense the general feelings of their respective parents. Therefore, if we are overly cautious or afraid to make decisions or take risks, our child will internalize this. Just as we took on some of our parents' thoughts and feelings so will our children. If there is a constant concern about health, wealth and popularity, the child also internalizes this. As parents, we want to examine how we react or feel in our day-to-day affairs. Parents need to be aware of their thoughts, feelings and responses in order to raise their children more effectively

Because of fear or doubt and parental intervention, many of us lost touch with our internal guidance systems. We do not trust ourselves to make good decisions. This lack of confidence stems from our significant others telling us what they feel is good or bad for us. The young however, tend to be more connected with who they truly are, and will follow and respond to their instincts or feelings. Their main focus is to be happy. They are aware that their life's purpose is to feel good and they spend their time playing, laughing and imagining.

Yet because of competitive lifestyles and the drive for success and fame, we often push our children to meet our expectations of what it means to be successful. We ignore their desires to live life and to learn from their mistakes, pain or joys. So, the more we push our children, the more they rebel, retreat or refuse our conditions, rules or judgments.

Tom And Kitty

Tom and Kitty are successful entrepreneurs who set high standards for their children aged 10 and 13. They demand excellent performance at school. Even when the children obtain high scores, both parents push harder and offer rewards for better grades. These children may be receiving the message that success is driven by external rewards. They may feel that there are conditions on their parents' approval and praise. There is a growing sense of conditional love here that could endanger the children's self-esteem and self-motivation. These children may live their lives in anguish because they will never enjoy their accomplishments. Because once they reach one goal, there is the constant push to excel at the next one. These children need to learn that there is nothing wrong with striving for the best, but that enjoying the journey is foremost. It is essential that they have fun and feel happy while succeeding in life. The children need to be loved and recognized no matter what grades they earn. Both Tom and Kitty need to trust that the children will do well and find success regardless of the external rewards offered to them. It is also important to note that both these children chose Tom and Kitty as their parents, thus highlighting that there is no blame here. These parents were probably driven by their parents to succeed and then continued the same behaviour that they endured as children and now continue to parent their children in the same manner.

We want our children to be perfect and to accomplish everything we did and many things we did not do. We don't accept them for who they are because we are always pushing them to achieve more or to do better. This causes incredible pressure upon them, causing them to feel unworthy and hopeless. Some parents withhold love or serve harsh punishments upon them when they don't achieve or when they make mistakes. Many make decisions for their children because they believe they know what is best for them. Meanwhile, these children become more withdrawn, impaired, afraid, anxious or defiant.

Kevin's Story

Kevin was in the first grade in school, and lived with his single mother. His father left them after he was born. Kevin was sad and suffered from depression. His mother worked long hard hours. She did the best she could to spend most of her free time with him, but he spent most of his time with a baby-sitter. This did not make Kevin feel good. He was having a hard time concentrating with the result he was not doing well in school, especially with his writing and reading.

His mother tried to help him read and write, but because most of the time she was tired, she was very impatient with him A friend of his mother visited quite often. She, on the other hand, sat and read with him and also found interesting fun things for him to do with the writing and reading. Kevin liked her approach and soon Kevin loved to read and write.

It is not that his mother did not want him to do well in school, but because her job demanded so much time and energy she did not have any left over for Kevin. Whereas her friend, who did not have a full-time job, had a strong desire to help Kevin.

Success depends upon how we feel when we do something. Kevin's mother was so very tired and worked with Kevin because she wanted him to do well in school, but she also felt a lot of guilt for having to leave Kevin with the baby-sitter so often. On the other hand, her friend loved Kevin and his mother, so she loved helping Kevin and his mother. Kevin's mother's friend's passion and eagerness to help him read inspired Kevin to do well.

Parents have difficult times dealing with teenagers when they are defiant and oppositional. As teens become increasingly estranged from their parents, they seek acceptance from their peers. Often they will turn to gangs in order to feel safe and accepted. As they struggle with issues of self-esteem, they may turn to bullying or violence in order to obtain their peers' approval. Others become victims of peer pressure, bullying or gang violence because they feel worthless or powerless. Some parents deal with these issues by imposing stricter rules or severer punishments. Others will give up and allow the children to leave home or to continue to indulge in reckless behaviour.

Remember that our children are our teachers. They are here to teach us how to love unconditionally. As parents, that is all we need to do. Prior to the teenage years parents need to provide reassurance and unconditional love to their children. Yet if we have not so far, it is never too late. Simply tell your children that you trust they will find their way and that we will provide support when needed. We must focus on anything that we can appreciate about them. In other words, ignore the difficult behaviours; trust that your child will find his/her way and that their decisions are right for them where they stand in their own lives. This is not to say that we do not communicate our opinions, beliefs or concerns with our children. Nor is it time to avoid setting rules and expectations. As parents we continue communicating our expectations allowing our children to voice their concerns and input. As we love, appreciate, respect and trust our teenagers, we will experience more harmony in the house.

Edward's Story

Edward grew up in a home were his parents were at war with each other. Their constant fighting frightened him. He would run and hide outside the house afraid that his father might come after him (which at times he did), when he wasn't physically abusing his mother. In search of solitude, he would run away from home and sleep on the streets. His father had nothing positive to say to Edward.

Due to all this negative reinforcement, Edward does not feel good about himself, he feels very insecure in simple social situations, and also has fits of rage and sometimes suffers from depression. Finally after years of arguments and abuse towards each other, the marriage broke up. Edward breathed a sigh of relief and he now knew he could go back home and enjoy the peace and quiet. But it was not long after he moved back home that Edward's father came back. Edward reacted with more anger and disruption. He acted out by staying out late and defying his parents. He would invite his friends over and they would leave the house in a mess. In her attempt to restore peace in the home, his mother called the police.

This infuriated Edward and he left home to live with his aunt. She loved him and he loved and respected her. She also respected him, she never judged him and she always saw the best in him. She encouraged and inspired him, and she knew that he would turn his life around. He started to go back to school and with her love and guidance he completed his schooling and started an apprentice program, putting his life together. Because of his aunt's love and complete faith in him, Edward regained his confidence and now continues to excel in all that that he does.

We need to help our children return to their spiritual core and be joyous We do this by teaching them to trust and listen to their inner emotions They learn by example, so we will demonstrate this living skill through our example of trusting our spiritual guide. They learn to effectively handle their challenges, by observing how we handle our challenges, when we get happy and find peace. Once we live this life skill, we must show them to examine how a situation makes them feel. We have taken them away from that inner knowing because we make too many choices for them. We provide them with advice to guide them, but we encourage them to choose what is good for them and what feels best to them. Letting their feelings guide them, our children learn to make their own choices in the world. If a situation does not feel good, then they need to reassess it and make changes that make them feel good. As we learned, when there are situations where we are unable to determine a clear choice, then the objective is to feel content and be patient. Start by expressing appreciation for someone or something. Then do something which makes them feel good. No one can make a decision if they are not feeling clear and content. Our obligation is to pass on our truth to them.

If we wish for our children to share their lives with us, we must truly listen to them. Know that our children, to the degree they are connected to their spiritual guide, will deal with their challenges and be fine. This is not to say that we just stand back and do nothing. Expressing how we feel and what we would do under their circumstances is fine, but respecting their decision is the key. Before we take action, we must discover whether or not our assistance will help our child further deal with the situation or whether we have disempowered them by taking over. Often we want to rescue our children and to save them from experiencing pain in life. We relive the pain we suffered in our youth when our children share their heartache with us. As soon as we lecture our children telling them what to do in these situations, we lose them.

Exercises

1) Trust that they have their own inner guidance and that they will find their way.

2) Focus only on the good that they do and ignore the rest.

3) Praise them when they do things that please you.

4) Help them to be in touch with how they are feeling and teach them how to trust what they feel.

5) Guide them through by showing them how you make decisions for yourself by trusting your emotional monitor.

Synopsis

Find any opportunity to praise, appreciate, love, honor, respect, and encourage your children. When we support our children, allowing them to make decisions for themselves along with our unbiased guidance; they will show us their brilliance, their trust and respect. The more we give them our full unconditional love the more they will make us proud parents.

Relationships with Friends

We attract friends into our lives the same way that we manifest other things. "Water seeks its own level" applies to friendships and other optional relationships. Our friendships may not always share common issues and experiences, which is the reason that brings you together. On the surface it may appear that you are very different from each other, but attraction comes through shared thoughts and feelings. Each friendship serves a purpose, either to support and validate us, or to challenge us. As in all of our relationships, friends act as mirrors of who we are, and what we believe in today.

Charlie And Lou's Story

Charlie and Lou were friends; both of them grew up having to fend for themselves. They lost their fathers at a very young age. Most of what they had accumulated in their lives was due to their hard work and struggle. Because of this upbringing they were both very controlling. They did not trust many people, but at the same time they had a tremendous need to be appreciated and admired. So what drew them together was the strange desire to be appreciated and also their fear of abandonment and their lack of trust.

The relationship had many ups and downs. When they were talking to each other things between them went well. They would hang out and do many thing they both enjoyed doing. These events though were short-lived. It was always one of them that would create something to anger the other. The underlying emotion here being, "I will leave you before you leave me." They continued these on-and-off encounters with each other until Charlie went to counseling. There, he realized that this is why they were not having the relationship they both desired, but could not seem to achieve.

Through this new awareness Charlie first told himself that he was now deserving of having many healthy happy relationships in his life and that he can start to trust more. He began to appreciate and trust himself more. He realized that he did not treat himself well. Due to his need for attention and admiration he allowed some people to take advantage of his needy nature. Once he changed these feelings about himself he noticed that his relationship with Lou grew stronger and they both treated each other with more respect.

They were both able to say no to each other and to others and not feel guilty or selfish for doing so. And it felt good to no longer do things just to feel needed.

Ilena And Susan's Story

Ilena and Susan socialized in the same circles, so there were many opportunities to be in each other's company Ilena was unhappy and depressed. Her father had left them when she was only three years of age. Her mother worked hard, long hours to provide for them. This left the children to fend for themselves. Ilena felt neglected, and not good about herself. Being a child of a broken home, she was ashamed. She used her insecure feeling to abuse and bully some of her friends at every opportunity.

Susan also felt insecure in many ways. Her brothers were constantly teasing her and telling her that she was stupid, ugly and made her feel that no one loved her. This made her very needy and desperate to get attention. Her parents were no comfort to her; they were too busy in their careers. So Susan became used to being treated with negativity and feeling like a victim.

So whenever Susan was in Ilena's presence, they argued and fought. Ilena pushed her around, and tried to pick fights with her. Ilena also called her terrible names and told her she was stupid and ugly. Ilena took out all of her frustrations and the pain she still felt about her parents breakup on Susan. Susan was an easy target because of her insecurities, and because she was used to being treated this way by her brothers.

It was not until Ilena went for counseling about her parents' separation that she came to terms and understanding of why she treated her friends the way she did.

By letting go of those shameful feelings around her parents' separation, she started to feel better about herself and her relationship with Susan improved.

When the changes took place within Ilena, her relationship with Susan improved. As a result, Susan started to feel better about herself; she liked how well she was now being treated by Ilena. She desired that all her other relationships feel the same way. Through this new intention that Susan set out for herself, she started to see positive changes in the way others started to communicate with her. Besides the great relationship that she and Ilena were now having, she also noticed that her brothers were appreciating her more. They no longer called her stupid and ugly. They treated her with more respect, and started to tell her that she was attractive. She now understood that her friends and her brothers could only treat her according to how she was feeling about herself. In this example, Ilena and Susan were both willing to take responsibility for their part in their relationship.

Synopsis

When we assess our lives and make changes, we may choose to leave some friendships, or some friendships may dissolve due to lack of attention by both parties. The essential element is to not end a friendship with anger or resentment. Having resentment will perpetuate the relationship, not heal it. We must examine and realize what the relationship brought to us. Upon parting, if there is any blame, anger or resentment, we will attract the same kinds of friendships again. When ending any relationship, we must appreciate our lessons learned and wish them well on their journey.

Exercises

Apply another joyous living skill and watch the miracles happen.
It does not matter how bad the relationship is or how long it has been this way, you have the power to change it by the following:

1) Be willing to take your attention off the problem. Ignore, ignore, ignore.

2) Only focus on the parts of them you like and appreciate that about them.

3) Start loving and appreciating yourself more. Do things to make yourself happy. IT IS NOT YOUR FRIEND'S RESPONSIBILITY TO MAKE YOU HAPPY.

4) Be willing to own your part in what is going wrong in the relationship What beliefs and feelings are we bringing into the relationship?

5) Be willing to see and feel about this relationship in a more positive light.

When we are happy, your partner can be happy with you.

6) Visualize the relationship the way you would like it to be, and feel good even though it is not yet the way you want it to be.

On The Job

Have you ever experienced anxiety and lack of energy when you prepare for work? Do you hate your colleagues? Do you dread every task? The relationships we create and experience in our workspace are also very important because, again, they mirror where we are in our own lives. We create the atmosphere in which we work. If we are negative and resentful, our workspace may be negative or difficult, causing us pain. When we engage in gossip, complaining or laying blame, we pass the responsibility of creating a positive workspace onto others. We must alter our attitudes about our work environment and colleagues in order to enjoy our jobs.

Often the work environment may be negative, but we must realize that it is a match to how we are feeling. If we shift our feelings, our work environment will shift or we will find a better workspace. Although it may be difficult to feel positive when faced with negative co-workers, we must appreciate the challenge they offer. Many of us choose to leave and find other employment, overlooking that we take ourselves with us. We take the negative feelings we have about this situation with us to the new job and eventually we create the same experience over again. An ineffective manager or disorganized colleague can show you aspects of yourself that you need to change in order to attract the effective manager or supportive colleague you deserve. Appreciate as much as you can in order to alter your experience and to move on to better and more prosperous employment.

Nancy's Story

Nancy worked in an office where her co-worker talked obsessively which was very distracting. What agitated her most was that this worker spoke mostly about other people's problems, her problems and her negativity towards her boss. Nancy worried about her family and she indulged in a lot of negative self talk. When this was pointed out to her, she knew that this person was reflecting back to her how she (Nancy) felt about herself.

When she became aware that this would continue until she thought more positively about herself, she started practicing positive thoughts and feelings. As soon as she did this, the co-worker talked less. She also become aware that on the days that she went to work worrying about her family or when she was not feeling good about herself, this worker was back to her negative talk.

Nancy now knows that this co-worker was a gift in her life to show her how she was thinking and feeling. She is at peace with the knowledge, it is never about them; it is always about how we are thinking and feeling.

Katherine's Story

Katherine hated her job. She complained constantly about her job, but realized that she needed the money to live. Through counseling she discovered the importance of appreciation of her job in any way possible. If she continued to feel that way, she would create a challenge of having to leave before she was ready to do so, or being fired. She looked for other work while finding some way to feel better about the job she had until the new job came. She made a list of the new jobs she wanted, and then she wrote a story and imagined herself enjoying all the things she wanted from this new job. Katherine began to find anything she could appreciate in her employment. Reminding herself that the job provided her with the money she needed to survive, Katherine began writing out lists of items she could appreciate about her co-workers and position. Finally, Katherine realized that her difficulty with all of her jobs stemmed from her lack of self-esteem and fear of failure. She kept finding employment that was simple and safe, but boring. Eventually, she found a management position due to her positive outlook and her new feelings of worthiness.

Synopsis

Remember the mirror we hold up for each other.
Remember we all have our story that we bring into the workplace.
Be willing to take them out of the box.
It is never about them, it is always about how we are thinking and feeling.
Change the feelings, then the relationship will change.
Ignore what is in front of you; find something happy to focus on.

Exercises

1) Write pages and pages of appreciative things about these people with whom you are having challenges.

2) Appreciate what you have about your job.

3) Write pages of things you like about yourself.

4) Write a letter telling about your friendships, and the wonderful people with whom you work.

5) Visualize having wonderful interactions with the people with whom you work. Do this not to change the relationship, but because it makes you feel good to imagine things going well in your life.

Love and Romance

Many of us experience challenges creating long-lasting loving relationships. Sometimes our significant partner's behaviour is difficult for us to accept. Our solution is to change them, as if we could. We believe that by changing the undesirable behaviour, we can create the perfect lifelong relationship. Conflict begins when your partner has no intention of changing. So, you remain angry and discontent for a lifetime of complaining about your partner. Many of my clients believe that they were not the problem in their problematic relationship. They believed happiness would occur if they received more flowers, more attention, or less hassle from their partner.

Many of my clients tell me that the new relationship they are in is different from previous ones. If the past relationship was physically abusive, then in the one they are in now, the man appears to be passive. I will point out to them that if they have not changed their thinking and feelings about themselves and what they thought about men when they were in the past relationship, what may appear to be different about this new relationship may not be the case. If you have not forgiven and let go of the past and your previous feelings, you will see evidence of similar behaviour. Instead of abuse, you will receive neglect. For you to attract a better relationship you have to change how you think and feel about yourself and your potential partners in general.

Many people live their lives repeating the same behaviour over and over again, attracting relationships that satisfy this pattern even though the person says "No, this is not what I want. I want to be happy." Nothing will change until they transform their thinking. They have to be willing to see and own their role in the creation. Nothing comes into our experience unless we are a match to these feelings and thoughts. Some of my clients needed to go back and revisit their past issues one more time. They received great value in returning to the place in their past which created the thoughts and feelings that are no longer appropriate. They examined it closely, and then shifted their consciousness, their beliefs and attitudes about how they had been living their lives. It is as though a light bulb goes on for them and they finally understand their thinking and feeling. They are then more willing to move forward. Freeing themselves, they stop the blame and guilt. Once the process starts it takes on a life of its own and soon they find themselves more peaceful, more loving, and more appreciative. They also see others around them in a different and more positive light. When they apply the power of the present to their new outlook of life, magically new and positive people come into their lives.

We have grown up in a world of victim consciousness. Someone is right and the other person is wrong. As soon as we accept and understand that as we think and feel we will attract and create, then there are no victims. People associate according to how they are thinking and feeling. Also, many of us have come here with a clear intention and agreements with others to share a particular experience. In all relationships we interact with people who are the same as ourselves. What may look like your opposite may actually turn out to be a reflection of your thoughts and feelings. If you examine your partner's beliefs and behaviours most certainly you will find some underlying beliefs and attitudes that you share. Our partner's behaviour tells us a great deal about who we are or how we are feeling. Telling us about the issues we have not yet dealt with, our partners inspire us to examine and then deal with them so we can move forward in our lives.

Donna's Story

Donna brought many of her own issues into the relationships she formed with men. Both her parents drank and her father barely held down a job. Her mother and father were mean when drinking and imparted harsh punishments upon the children. Donna felt that her father was irresponsible and he was, in fact, unfaithful to her mother and often physically and emotionally abusive to the whole family. Donna recalled the odd time when he was endearing. She sat on his lap for a drawing contest. Her father teased her, telling her she would amount to nothing in art. Because of her determination to prove him wrong she became a talented professional artist.

Donna and her younger siblings grew up with conflicting beliefs. Their father expressed that women were not to be trusted, while her mother warned them not to trust men. For years they were exposed to constant fighting and substance abuse. Donna's older sibling left home when she was 10 years of age. Donna worked at part-time jobs in the evening helping her mother clean offices. At home, Donna would start dinners at night, clean the home and care for the youngest sibling. She was not allowed out to play with other children and had to stay home all the time.

In her adult life, Donna chose partners who also had alcohol and drug addictions. She suffered two broken marriages because of her partners' lack of support and Donna's own alcohol problem. Despite her desire for a family and a loving relationship, Donna's own sadness and desperation led her into a spiral of failure with men. She did experience success in her own business; however, each time she separated from a mate she chose to leave everything behind.

Her fear of losing people she loved created a great deal of pain. For example, Donna created some health issues in her life because she chose to hold on to the pain and grief of her past. This health problem resulted in major surgery. By seeking help, she began to turn this around. With a great deal of determination, Donna began to make some progress through counseling. She learned to get to know herself better and to release her past pain through exercises and workshops. She learned that the point of power is in the present moment.

We always have choice: when we are standing in a place that does not feel good; we can continue to focus in that direction and receive more of the same. Or we can turn our attention, our thoughts and our feelings to what we would now want from this situation. Find the thought and/or feeling that will help us to move more into the direction of what we would like to receive from this challenge. Right now, we get to choose.

It does not matter how bad the situation is or how long we have been living with this challenge. Right now we can decide to continue to worry, be angry and negative or we can find some way to soothe the feelings. If remaining angry for now makes you feel a little better, then be angry, but you may not want to stay there for too long because the aim is to find some way to ultimately transform that feeling into something that makes you feel better. When you do this now, in the future if this situation remerges, you have an experience that is more in line with what you want and the tools to get it.

Donna realized that she had a choice and this would free her from the past pain she had chosen to retain. She chose to become more loving and kind to herself and to others. Donna began to channel much of her pain into creative avenues, transforming the negative into positive. She changed her perception by learning to transform stumbling blocks into stepping stones. Her decision to acknowledge her past and her role in attracting different situations and events was her choice to be free of her pain in the future. Her acceptance and also her strong desire and willingness to move forward has resulted in her body now starting to heal.

Uri And Dee's Story

Uri and Dee met when they were in their twenties. Both had experienced many relationships. They came into the relationship with similar emotional issues. They were looking and hoping to find a mate that would make them happy. Uri had low self-esteem created in his childhood, perpetuated in later relationships by abusive partners, while Dee also experienced challenges with her self-worth because of what she had perceived as competitive parents. These people also experienced trust issues with the opposite sex due to past abandonment and pain.

How could this ultimately be a happy, healthy relationship? Uri and Dee relied on each other to feel good about themselves. They truly believed that a relationship would heal their issues and provide them with bliss. If Uri and Dee did not love themselves, how could they love someone else? In time, the relationship became strained as each of them set conditions upon the other. Uri was not attentive enough. This behaviour triggered Dee's neediness and abandonment issues.

Eventually Dee went for counseling and through this work she realized that for this relationship to change she has to own her part in this manifestation. That as long as she held all these negative feelings about herself and the relationship, nothing was going to change for her. She was given exercises to change how she felt about herself. One of those exercises was to write pages and pages of positive statements about herself. Also, to list things about herself she appreciated. Then she wrote things about Uri that she could appreciate. She wrote a story about them enjoying a wonderful happy relationship in the past.

Uri and Dee were looking outward for happiness and satisfaction. They depended upon each other for filling the voids they had inside themselves. Uri and Dee needed to fix their own issues separately. Dee needed to love herself first so that she would stop relying upon Uri to make her feel good and important. Also, Uri needed to feel good about himself, so that he could give unconditionally without feeling threatened. Uri needed to trust that whatever he provided Dee would be enough and unconditional. They needed to love themselves first so that they could love one another.

We need to claim ownership whenever there is discord in a marriage or union. For example, when your mate approaches you in an angry fashion, examine what your feelings are that attracted this. Perhaps you are feeling angry over some other issue or are in a negative space. Constant complaining about a partner is also detrimental to your relationship. The more we focus on the negative behaviour, the more it surrounds us. Few relationships can change if we are constantly laying blame and complaining. If we want happy relationships, we need to get happy first. Examine your behaviour in the relationship and ask yourself if you could handle your attitudes or behaviours! Begin by taking care of yourself, then enjoy a new or renewed pastime. In this way, you will be shifting your attention from the negative behaviour of your partner. Eventually your partner will either join you in your new space or you will find a closer match for the new you!

Some of us, however, wish to work on the relationship using appreciation. We spend so much time and energy focusing on negative behaviour, that we forget the characteristics we once loved and appreciated. Many relationships improve if we focus upon any one characteristic or event that is joyous. Whatever it takes, focusing on their children or the early days of their courtship, we must turn our attention away from the negative and focus on anything we can appreciate about each other.

I recall a woman who attended one of my workshops and said that she had had a very bitter separation from her husband. They had not talked for many years. Most interaction and communication was done through their children. But during the class, she realized her part in creating this unhealthy relationship. She was willing to take responsibility for it. By applying some of the skills of appreciation and understanding, she was able to examine the past and her ex-husband in a different light. A few weeks after the class, her ex-husband called the house. She answered the phone and for the first time in many years, they spoke in a civil fashion.

When this woman changed her attitude and beliefs about the relationship, meaning she took ownership for her part in its rupture, she was able to find completion. She clearly understood how this relationship had failed to provide her with what she wanted. This was due to her negative thoughts and feelings. She also realized her years of trying to make him change, so that she could be happy, had not been the answer. What was needed was for her to change herself first.

You can start today, right now, to shift your feelings from negative to positive; then we are able to alter the manner in which our friends, co-workers, children and partners approach us. Eventually, through self- love and appreciation, we can come to feeling more joyous and therefore bring new people into our lives that are similar to us.

One of my clients expressed her experience very well:

"Now that I have the tools of putting a stop to my negative thoughts and quickly replacing them with a good feeling or a positive thought, I have the power and responsibility of my world. Every thought is powerful. I envisioned myself happy and loving with my husband.

I allowed myself only to focus upon his good qualities and I literally found myself laughing aloud to myself as I remembered what I admired most about him. Did this ever feel good, what a release! Eventually our communication became more tender and gentle. I began to focus upon positive thoughts of traveling and riding a white horse along the seashore. Incredibly, after 16 years of marriage, he calls me up one afternoon and surprised me with a trip to Cuba for our anniversary. I obviously accepted the trip and a week later we found ourselves away from our responsibilities and our children for the first time. Needless to say, as I continue to incorporate the skills I have learned to appreciate my life, me and those around me; I have found happiness anew in my marriage." K.W.

Strategies

1) Focus more on the good things about the other person, people.

2) Remember the times when you were happy.

3) Find things to appreciate about them.

4) Take your attention off of the marriage and find other things that make you feel good to think and focus on.

5) Remember the times when you first met.

Relationship Exercises

1) Write some positive things about yourself and the people in your life.

2) Write things you appreciate about them. Even if you can think of only one thing about them to appreciate, that is what you need to focus on when you think about them.

3) If you put your focus in a more appreciative place, the relationship must change. Or because they are no longer a match to you, the universe will bring you a more compatible partner because you have changed your vibration or your thinking. Because of changing your thinking you changed how you feel about this person and this relationship.

4) If this relationship is not worth the effort for you to change, change how you feel anyway so that you can attract something different, either in this relationship or to allow a new and better one to come.

5) If you want to have a happy relationship you have to get happy first. If you do not get happy and remain miserable, your higher self can only bring you another unhappy, miserable person. This is universal law.

6) You cannot have a happy relationship if you do not feel worthy of one.

Items to Remember:

1) Ask for what you want about these relationships.

2) Start living and acting as if you already have what you asked for.

3) Trust that what you now asked for is on its way to you.

Feeling good is everything. You get to choose where you place your attention: on happy thoughts and feelings or negative thoughts and feelings. The Point of Power is Now!

Synopsis

The good news is you can have a good relationship, but the catch is you will have to do the work. Get happy first and any relationship can improve or change. When you get happy, you'll form more fun-loving friendships. The people in our lives share our belief systems, levels of self-esteem and issues. Looking carefully, we note the mirror image of parts of ourselves in the people around us. Remember to appreciate yourself and appreciate them for the gift they are showing you.

As we discussed, the most important part of our relationships is our relationship with ourselves. We must be willing to take responsibility for our part in the events and situations that show up in our lives. So always start in the beginning, with the face in the mirror.

Relationships Visualization

Create a Goals List about what you want in your relationships. This could be your interaction with your significant other, your family, your children, your friends, or any other relationship. Let your imagination go and create all the details of what you want in your future. Write it down before you do the visualization.

Bring into the visualization all those aspects of the person that you would like to have. If it is that you want someone who is a good listener, see him/her interact with you being attentive and interested in what you have to say. If you want someone who is playful and healthy with lots of energy, see the two of you doing playful things and visualize his/her strong, healthy body. These are just some examples to get you started.

Most importantly do this exercise for the fun of it, NOT to create an outcome. You do this visualization just because it makes you feel good to go there. Then and only then can this partner come. Make this feel so real as if you are already enjoying such an experience.

Relationships Visualization

Find a comfortable place to lie down. You may want to play some music and have a blanket to cover you.

Do whatever you need to do to feel at ease. Take in 4 deep breaths, hold the breath for the count of 4 and then exhale for the count of 4. Now take in 5 long deep breaths, hold them for the count of 5, and then exhale for the count of 5. Now take another last breath and breathe it out while feeling the body soften even more. With this exhalation, let go of any distracting thoughts and emotions.

Now imagine yourself in one of these relationships. See yourself interacting with this person or persons. Feeling the joy that it is to be with the person, how much fun you have, doing playful things. If it is your significant relationship, you may want to visualize their strong and healthy body. You may imagine yourselves running along the beach with your dog.

Or maybe you are with a friend, a very good friend, see yourselves sitting and enjoying each other's company. Feel the mutual respect you have for each other. Or you may be thinking about your parents. See them happy and healthy, busy with their own lives. You love them and they love you. Communicating and feeling the respect you have for each other. And this goes for all relationships. That anything they say or do, you acknowledge that this is who they are, and we allow them to be how they are. Recognize that we all have our story, our challenges and that we deal with our situation in our own way. There is no judgment; we allow each other to live their lives even if it is not the one we would like for them.

If you are focusing on the children, you may want to see them in the classrooms, happy to be there. Alert and eager to learn, or you may want to see them involved in a hobby they love, or being with their friends having fun. Or you may be seeing yourself sitting and having a meal with them. Everyone happy and relaxed, enjoying each other's company, having great conversation and a lot of laughter.

You could be imagining the whole family together participating in a particular action. It could be riding your bike, watching a movie, going on a picnic. Everyone is happy and enjoying themselves, you can feel the respect and adoration amongst each other. The humour and bantering with each other, this could also apply to all your other relationships.

You could also have some more intimate moments with your significant partner. You could visualize getting all dressed up to go on a special date; you are feeling very excited and passionate about having this interaction and being with the special person in your life. Knowing that all the plans and preparing you did is now finally going to unfold exactly as you imagined. You may be seeing yourselves in a beautiful restaurant, having an intimate and loving discussion. You are feeling beautiful and they look amazing also.

Then you could see yourself interacting with a parent/parents, everyone together feeling relaxed and happy to be together with a lot of mutual respect. It does not matter what they say or do not say. You just allow them to be who they are; there is no judgment or wanting them to be a certain way

If it is a work situation, you may see yourself interacting with these people, everyone doing their work. You have great relations with these people, everyone respecting each other. Or it could be that you now have a new job working with creative happy people. Like you, they love their jobs. Coming to work is fun and stimulates their individual talents and many profitable ideas. Everyone respects and admires each other's talents. They love coming to work to express and share their individual ideas.

If there are people you may have some challenges with, you therefore do not have too much interaction with them. You have decided you will respect them for who they are, understand that just as you have your story so do they. And you also know that if you have an unpleasant experience with them, that they are showing you something about yourself that you need to own. So just love them and see them becoming happier people.

Then you may want to see yourself five years from now living a happy joyful life. Your body is just the way you would like it to be, you have a great job that you love, and your relationships are healthy. You have your perfect mate, you have a fabulous job, and you may even have your own business. Everyone gets along well at your job. Money is flowing in and you feel very prosperous. It may not be as much as you would like to have, but you have the inner knowing that all is well in your life and the most important key for you is to stay happy.

See yourself going through your day and interacting with some of your staff and how great you feel when you leave your workplace, you cannot wait to get back the next day. Life is just wonderful.

Then you may want to fast-forward and see yourself 10 years from now. You may be in a new location or a new home. You may have sold your business and are doing something different with your life. Or still in the same company doing extremely well, moving forward, you are appreciative of all your wonderful friends, maybe have new friendships, and some of your past friends have moved on with their life. Everyone is happy and enjoying life and wishing each other well in their endeavors.

Your parents have aged, but are in good health and happy and are pretty amazing with all their activities and hobbies. Plus your children (if you have any) are grown and have great jobs, some of them have moved away, gotten married and all are living their lives. No matter what it is they are doing with their lives, you trust that they will find their way. Many times they have shown you that you can trust them to do what is right for them.

You may want to start to come back. You feel relaxed, happy and ready to have happy satisfying interaction in your future relationships. You have picked up a few ideas that you want to include in your relationships or some specific interaction.

Exercises

1) You may want to journal some of your feelings from the meditation.

2) Draw the images you saw that will help the relationship.

3) You may have been inspired to write an appreciative letter or card.

4) For those you may still have challenges around, you may want to not think about this relationship. Think only about those relationships that are doing well.

5) Invoke and tell the source what you would like to have in this challenging friendship. You want to find a comfortable way to be in a relationship with this person that makes you both feel good. Then let the universe guide you and show you the way. Let the universe take care the rest.

6) Find one thing about this person you can appreciate. Maybe they always dress nicely or you like the way they wear their hair, and then only focus on the part of them that pleases you.

7) If that is too difficult only focus and think about situations and events that make you feel good.

Student comments

"I have more joy in my life and I understand that it is only I that can control that. If I am not feeling joy, I now know what I need to do to feel joy. My relationship with my family and my business relationships has improved greatly. I can say that I am a much happier balanced person. However, I also know that I have only reached a small fraction of what I can be and therefore I will continue my practices and I thank Marlene for introducing these teachings to me and for always being there to support and guide me when necessary." K. E.

"I have healed a past relationship with my daughter's father. I am happier, more appreciative, loving myself more and now I can love him unconditionally. He gave me a beautiful daughter. She is autistic and very sensitive to how I am feeling. If I had a bad day she would react negatively towards me. She is my greatest teacher.

Now that I am much happier and have released the hurts around my relationship with her father, my daughter and I are becoming so much closer. Our interactions are more positive and I am noticing major positive growth changes in her.

Thank you Marlene, you have shown me many ways to heal, and to be more appreciative of myself and others." T. S.

chapter Six

Forgiveness

Joyous Living Skill #6: Be willing to own your own part in your relationships. There is no need to forgive.

Through forgiveness we allow more joy and harmony into our lives. If this is not what you have in your life right now you may want to take a look and see who you need to forgive. It may mean that you need to forgive yourself for the part you played.

Many of my clients who come to me with challenges in relationships say "I have forgiven." But the very person they say they have forgiven is the person we are discussing in the session. For many, forgiveness has been an intellectual experience. For some, conditions were placed on the person they were forgiving. "I will forgive you if..." This form of forgiveness did not change how they felt about the person. All the negative feelings that they have harboured over the years have not changed. You will know if you have forgiven the person, or persons, if you can be with them and allow them to be themselves. There is no judgment on your part, wanting them to be different. We accept them for who they are and love them no matter what the challenge. People treat each other badly because they are in their own pain. Once you understand their story, the life they lived, you have the information and understanding of why they act the way they do, the choices they make.

No one can make us feel angry or feel jealous. We take on those emotions and we label them. As long as we feel that someone has treated us unjustly, we cannot free ourselves from this feeling of wrongdoing and blame. We have to release these thoughts from our consciousness. This, in turn, will change how we feel about the situation and the person we believe is causing the pain.

If this is not done you will draw into your life people and events that will be similar to those past situations and you will find yourself experiencing that same past situation over and over again. It does not matter if the person is dead or alive, these people are chained to us. You will be drawn into situations that are matching your thoughts and feelings You can buy the bigger home, move to another country, win the lottery; it doesn't help. You will take these people with you because of your thoughts and feelings about them and what you perceive was done to you.

In forgiving them we are not doing them a favour. In fact, they may not even care. However, we are doing ourselves a wonderful service. We deserve to be happy, and no one can be truly happy harbouring anger or resentment. Even if the cause of our negative feelings is dead, by changing our feelings toward that person we can change our lives. Experience the power of the present as soon as you flip the switch from resentment to acceptance when thinking about the departed soul who caused you so much pain. Like an old bandage wrapped around your heart, squeezing the life out of it, resentment threatens your very existence. As soon as you release your negative feelings toward the person, you'll feel the bandage unwrap your heart, allowing it to expand and embrace all the love that is already in your life.

There are no exceptions to forgiveness, there are no levels to forgiveness. There are no unforgivable sins. Remember, you made a contract with all of the people in your life to teach you lessons about love and acceptance. Even the people who wronged you did so living out their part in your relationship. They were just doing their job, as you are doing yours. It's not the acts that continue to hurt you, it's your unwillingness to let go of the pain associated with those acts. Hurtful as they were, the only person they hurt now is you because of your reluctance to move beyond them. Turn the page on what you don't want, and prepare yourself for a life of what you do want when you forgive those who've given you pain in the past.

For instance, if you were in a relationship with an alcoholic who physically abused you, you leave that relationship. If you do not heal that past relationship, by that I mean take ownership for your part in it, you will only attract a similar relationship in the future. To move forward we have to change how we felt about the relationship. If you felt victimized, then you can only attract another relationship in which you will feel like a victim. In your new relationship the person may not drink, but he/she abuses you verbally. For instance, they may be sober, yet they insult you in front of your children, friends and in public places. By not clearing up your negative feelings about the earlier relationship through forgiveness, you bring the "victim" self-image into all the succeeding relationships. The first step is to clean up your own act, own your part in the past, accept the abuser for who he was - someone to teach you lessons you needed to learn - forgive both of you and no longer be a victim, so you can move on to a better life.

Remember what was discussed in the relationship chapter: that we come into relationships with each other, each with our own story. We only come together because in many ways we are similar. For instance, if this person who is abusing you does not love him/herself, there must be something about you that is not loving yourself either. You may allow others to place demands on you, which may reflect the demands you place upon yourself. By changing how you feel about them, your life becomes more harmonious, peaceful and joyful.

How do we go about healing this? We need to stop the blame, the guilt and to stop transferring our pain onto them. It does not matter what caused the problem, we can move forward if we really want to get on with our lives. It is our commitment and willingness to heal that relationship that will free us so that we can live the life of joy, peace, harmony and prosperity that we all deserve.

We only need to state our desire once, and then have no doubt that the relationship can be healed. For instance, "Universe, I am willing to find a way to forgive myself for the role I played in this relationship and I am now ready to move forward. Please show me the way to do this." But some of us prefer to be right rather than being happy. In this way, we justify why we are not forgiving.

Another example is: "I am an abused child." Because this is what we are thinking and feeling we place ourselves in relationships where the abuse continues. It either shows up as physical, emotional or spiritual abuse.

Another example is if you were an abandoned child and you place yourself in situations where you feel abandoned and create events where people will leave you. Some will take the position where they will leave the relationship before the other person leaves them. In this way, we sabotage the relationship. Through this choice we may be abusing ourselves.

This is not about right or wrong. We deserve to have loving caring people around us. It is not about them forgiving us so much as it is about us forgiving us, so that we can free ourselves and move on with our lives. Stop blaming others for what we are creating.

My Story

When I look back into my life I now see how perfect it all was; how my higher self was guiding me every step of the way.

My belief as a little girl was that my father did not love me. This was my perception and I labeled it as rejection. If you were to ask my sisters, they have a different impression as to how they felt growing up in our household. I also believed that my parents were not there for me emotionally, so I created a health challenge for myself with anorexia. I starved myself for days. Anorexia is a form of self-hatred. Through all of this I controlled my family. Dinnertime at our home was a nightmare. Everyone was focused on me, because I did not want to eat. But through all of this I had been given concentrated negative attention. At least this made me feel I was being noticed, even for the wrong reasons.

When I married Colin, my husband, I placed him in the role of my father. I clung to my belief that men reject me and men are not there for me emotionally. With the result, I attracted a man who could not provide me with the emotional support I needed. Because of his upbringing, and his trust issues about women, he could not respond in the way I would have liked.

At one point in our marriage, I thought I had tried everything to make this marriage work, and yet we had challenges. First, I went for counseling, and then we both went for counseling, but nothing changed. I felt desperate and lonely. My belief was if he would change, I would be happy. I believed in God, I had attended Catholic school and went to the Anglican Church, I did everything I thought I was supposed to do to have a happy marriage. Still, I wanted to control it; I wanted to be in charge. This attitude was not serving me anymore and I was becoming more and more depressed and unhappy. Then one day, in desperation I fell down on my knees in pain, shouting: "God if it is me, please change me." At that time in my life, I still believed that outside powers had to change things for me. I did not realize that it was all about how I was thinking and feeling about this relationship that made the difference. I needed to change my perceptions and beliefs about this marriage. Only then could things improve. The asking was important. That was the first step to receiving something different in my marriage. Also my strong desire to have a happier marriage and my willingness to release all the negative feelings I held about this relationship. I remember after asking, I felt a sense of peace. I knew that everything was going to be OK. I had no doubt things would change for me.

And things did change within me. After this incident, I felt more peaceful. All the negative feelings left me. I was guided to enroll in a university program and joined a community theatre group.

I realized what I had been doing. I was placing Colin in the role of my dad, wanting him to make me happy. Until I was willing to forgive myself, Colin, and my parents, my relationship and my perception of what I believed they did to me was not going to change. My parents did the best they could under the circumstances. They were in their pain and they were caught up in their story and their past. I, on the other hand, saw myself as a victim of my past.

The sad part about this is that many of us pass our stories on to our children. Or what we blame our parents for, we do to ourselves or to others. I was not there for me emotionally. I rejected me. Anorexia was a form of self-hatred. I was denying my own existence.

Some of us go in the opposite direction. Because no one was there for us, we smother, and therefore cripple, our children. That is another way of dumping our stuff on others. I was not there for my son the first 15 years of his life. I was so caught up in my own pain that I did not know how to be there for him emotionally. This was due to my life experience. It was a learned behaviour.

So it is not so much about forgiving the other people in our lives, although they may have done something really horrible. This is about freeing ourselves so that we can turn our attention to what we want out of life. More love, more peace and more happiness.

We need to break the patterns of identity like the ones I had: "Men reject me. Men aren't there for me emotionally. I cannot trust them." Because of these belief and feelings about the significant men in my life I set myself up to be rejected and attracted men that did not support me emotionally. The incident may only have occurred once, but we keep punishing ourselves and others over and over again. The abused becomes the abuser.

Dana's Story

Dana was only five years old when her father died as the result of a traffic accident. Her mother had many men in her life as Dana matured. Her mother introduced most of these men as Dana's future father, which never seemed to happen. As soon as Dana became attached to any of them, her mother would move on to the next one. During elementary school, Dana's mother married one of her men, a divorced father of two sons. The boys were older than Dana, so she was left in their care often when the parents went out socializing. It wasn't long before she was being sexually abused by her stepbrothers. Eventually her mother tired of her stepfather and divorced him. During her teenaged years, Dana became anorexic which is often the result of family sexual abuse. Dana told her therapist she felt her body was the only thing in her life she could control. As she matured she felt certain that all the men in her life would either leave or abuse her, and of course they did. She used them as an excuse for her adult alcoholism. A friend recommended one of my workshops, during which she realized her part in her own story. After committing to a better life, she did the work to free herself of the anger she held against her father for abandoning her, her mother for not protecting her from her boyfriends and stepbrothers, and finally herself for the guilt she felt in all of it.

Many of us believe that dis-ease in the body is a mental and spiritual imbalance. Consider my experience with anorexia. As long as I held on to thinking about my parents and that they were not there for me emotionally, I would continue to have the challenge. As long as I wanted to be right and in charge, nothing could change. As soon as I was ready to forgive them my life changed.

Current research has found that, if we have a stressful thought, the muscles in the body contract. But if we add more joyful thoughts about the body, our muscles relax thereby improving our health.

As we will discuss in Chapter Seven on Health, the body follows the mind, meaning if you worry about your health issue the body cannot heal. But when you think positive thoughts about your body, your body will start to recover.

Nothing has power over us. We give it power. We either empower ourselves with our thoughts or we kill ourselves with our thoughts. Regardless of all the surface remedies we may take to alleviate pain, unless we are willing to free ourselves from these negative thoughts then illness, challenging conditions or other health issues will occur.

Abnormal tumors and cancers are the result of deep depression and anxiety. When we bypass this Law of Forgiveness (See Health, Chapter Seven) we bypass health. If we are living in the past we are dead. So what is keeping you stuck? Do not say you have forgiven if you have not; I've been there. It does not feel good. You are just holding yourself back from all the wonderful things you know you want.

We need to get in touch with our feelings and we need to understand why we repeat patterns in our lives over and over and over again. We must be willing to drop the blame, and stop projecting our pain onto others. We need to take back our lives and be willing to take responsibility for what we have manifested into our lives.

When you change your relationship with yourself you change all other relationships. When one person in the family heals it is possible for others in the family to also change for the better. There are those who do not want to forgive. We do not have to judge them. They have the right to live their life the way they choose. We do not have to be around them and continue to be abused by them. If you can, send them loving thoughts. If it is difficult for you to do that, think of anything else that makes you feel good. Then bless them on their journey and return to living your own life, your own positive way. Now watch your life getting better and better.

It does not matter how many enlightened books I have read, how many tapes and workshops I have attended or how much I meditate; if I have not forgiven myself and others, I will not have the peace and the joy I am looking for in my life. If you want to stop the wars, start with yourself. We are so wrapped up in our pain, that we forget what we have come here to do which is to be a lover. We are loving, caring beings. Forgive, release and let go. Make room for your source, your higher self. Let go of your frustrations, guilt and blame and let your spirit shine. We deserve to have it all. This is our birthright.

The challenge with this is once you give yourself permission to go back and revisit these issues, you do not stay stuck back there in those old negative feelings. I offer a workshop to my clients called "Learning to Move Forward." The power in this class is that it helps the student realize how their beliefs, thoughts and feelings have played out in their lives. In addition, the students learn that nothing will change until they are willing to take responsibility for their part in what they are attracting. Then the class provides them with the skills to make the changes they now want in their life. We need to be willing to forget about what happened and to change how we feel about the situations. Once we change how we feel, it becomes easier to forget. We can change the intense, angry thoughts to a frustrating thought; any thought, that is, which feels more comfortable than the original emotions surrounding the topic. The energy is where we last left it, and as we now know, we attract according to how we think and feel. Therefore, we change the thoughts and feelings, replacing them with more soothing thoughts and feelings about the subject. The experience that we blamed for holding us hostage will no longer have so much power over how we now feel about the event.

Debra's Story

Debra's life journey started when her sister was murdered by her brother-in-law, who then took his own life. This experience forced her to deal with death, loss and forgiveness. Once all the work was completed regarding the funeral arrangements and the gathering and clearing of their belongings, Debra was faced with the decision of how she was going to live her life after the death of her sister and the suicide of the brother-in-law. It took many months for the shock of this situation to wear off. Debra suffered many days with a heavy heart full of pain, and nights with nightmares. Normal everyday things, like a siren from a police cruiser, brought up a lot of fear. Eventually she went back to work and started to re-evaluate her life. She asked herself the question, "What really matters in my life now?" Meaning: Does my corporate job matter? Do all the toys matter? Does driving a nice car matter? Does living in a fancy home matter? Does wearing nice clothes matter? What is really important here?

At the same time, she saw her family struggling with their emotions. She wanted to support them, too. No one could even say the word "murder." Debra also wanted to find some answers for herself such as "Why did this happen to this family?" and "Why do people have to live with these heavy hearts and painful experiences?"

Eventually she saw her family moving on with their lives in their own way. Debra decided to quit her job and to travel. The purpose of her traveling was to continue her search for answers as to why this happened to her sister, and what she had to learn from this, and what she could do about it. During her travels through Europe, there was always a part of her searching for her sister. When she moved through the crowds at the train station, or while sitting on the coach, she longed to see her sister's face.

The next significant thing that came out of this experience was that a minister invited her to go into the prison to support the inmates with their challenges. She was to sit and meditate with those who had done similar deeds. Before she responded she asked herself, "If my brother-in-law was still alive would I want to go into the prison to help these inmates?"

Because Debra had been doing some of her own healing, she knew that this was something she had to do in order to find completion with the situation. Debra was part of the prison ministry for about 5 years. Towards the end of the second year Debra felt the impulse to share her story with the inmates. Many questions arose from her sharing. One being, "Why are you bothering to come here?" Debra's response was that she came to help herself with her unresolved emotional pain around the tragedy that was affecting her heart. As Debra shared her story, she observed their faces, heard and saw the pain in their eyes. Through sharing her story and their questions and noticing their trauma, Debra concluded that she attracted this experience of volunteering in the prison so that she could come to a place of complete forgiveness. Forgiveness for herself first, because all the hatred, resentment and anger she held towards her brother-in-law had resulted in poor emotional and physical health Then she needed to forgive her brother-in-law and others like some of the inmates who had committed similar acts.

Debra felt within her being that she had to release herself and them from their pain. She realized that they were in some way connected to her, meaning that, "We may look like individuals, but we are all one."

Because I was a part of this prison ministry for over 7 years, and the inmates were aware of my work, I offered to do a workshop at that time called "Transforming Anger" to help some of the inmates release their emotional pain. It was during this class that Debra had the opportunity to confront her own experience through speaking to an inmate who had done the same act. Debra acted as the mother of the girl that he murdered. Because much of the hurt and unpleasant memories surfaced while this process was unfolding, Debra at first was insistent that she, as the mother, was not willing to forgive this person. Her words were "There will be no forgiveness." At that moment, Debra knew that the mother of the girl that this inmate killed was holding herself back from having a happy life. Also, the inmate needed to forgive himself in order to find peace within. If he continued to feel the shame and guilt about what he did, he would continue to attract other situations and events that would confirm to him that he was, and still is, a bad person

As the session unfolded and she heard the inmate's childhood story, she felt empathy for him. She realized that her brother-in-law must have had a story and that his childhood contributed to his final act and the taking of his wife's life. Debra now knew that the time had come for her to truly release and forgive her brother-in-law.

On the other hand, her sister had her own challenges and issues. In many ways, before her death, she was heading down a path of self-destruction. Over the years, through Debra's learning and her understanding of how attraction works, she realized that these two were a match to what they finally co-created together. She also understood that her sister chose this avenue to free herself from her pain.

Debra now realizes that her sister's death taught her that when she is standing at a crossroad, she can choose life or death. Her sister helped Debra say yes to life. Debra has applied this learning many times. Since then, Debra has been challenged with a health crisis and she decided to manifest a healthy body over one that was deteriorating. At the same time, Debra does not judge her sister for the way she decided to end her life.

After that realization, doors started to open for her. She has been invited to share this experience with many. Debra plans to write a book based on this journey.

Ivan's Story

At one of my Healing Circles, one cold winter evening in 1987, the door flung open just before our break that evening. There in the doorway stood a gentleman. I could tell he was intoxicated. Everyone in the class now had their attention on our visitor, and were wondering what I was going to do about this person. I asked one of the ladies to go over to him and see what he wanted. She stood frozen in her place. I had to ask her a second time to go over and see what he wanted. Reluctantly, she went over to him. In the meantime, all eyes were on our visitor. I could tell he was not willing to leave so I called to her to bring him over to join the group. We were about 5 minutes from our break and I felt I could encourage him to leave during this break. He sat down and joined the group. I asked him for his name and he told us. We could all smell that he had been drinking. I could tell by their expressions some in the group were wondering why I invited him to stay. As we continued the class he made all kinds of grunting sounds as if he were acknowledging our conversation.

I told the visitor we were about to have our coffee break, and asked "Would he like to join us?" He said yes. I then asked for someone in the group to offer to take him downstairs and give him a beverage. No one responded. Finally, someone offered to escort the visitor.

The group went downstairs for their break, and as often happens someone would come to me during the break to converse with me. I was so involved with this person I forgot about our visitor, and that I intended to find a way to get him to leave.

The group returned and with them was our visitor. At this point in the class we generally do a group healing. This is accomplished with some students lying on the floor or sitting on the floor. I said to our visitor "We are now going to do a healing exercise and would you like to join us in some healing?" He went down on the carpet and to my amazement he laid down exactly as we have done over the years. He knew exactly how to position himself. No one wanted to lie next to him, because we generally hold hands. Reluctantly the gentleman that took him down for the break and the girl that greeted the visitor lay down on either side of him. We started our session: the lights were low and relaxing music lulled everyone into a meditative state. We were no more than a few minutes into the session when he started to speak. I went over to him and requested that he please be quiet. I barely left his side when he started speaking again. Again I asked him to be quiet, but at this point the most profound words came pouring out of his mouth. He spoke of trust, confidence, commitment, self-worth, strength, faith, passion, honesty, love, anger, appreciation, health, relationships and much, much more. He expressed the need to forgive by forgetting. About getting happy and finding our bliss. About our willingness to change our thinking. To find a way to soften the hold on our thoughts by softening the thinking. He continued this monologue for at least a half an hour. The class and I were spellbound. I could not believe that these words of wisdom were coming out of this man's mouth. At the end of the session, long after the music stopped playing, everyone sat in silence replaying in our minds what he had said. Many also felt sensations pouring through their bodies. When everyone finally drew themselves out of this trance he announced he was leaving.

When he said goodnight he stared directly into everyone's eyes. He held our gaze for a few minutes, as he bowed and placed his hands in the prayer position. When he had acknowledged us all, he turned to leave. Almost in unison, we said goodnight to him. I asked the girl who greeted him to guide him out the side door. He refused and told her he wanted to leave by the door he entered, because he had left his wine bottle outside that door.

After he left, many in the group shared how he had come and reminded them of things from their past or had provided them the answer to a challenge they were facing. For instance, the girl that greeted him said, "When he came through that door I was reminded of my father." Through his presence that night she was able to release some unresolved things she had with regard to her relationship with her father. The man who took him down for coffee was having challenges recently about his drinking. During the healing exercise, the visitor kept squeezing his hand saying: "You've got to have faith. Have courage, know that you can do it, you can conquer anything." These were the exact words he needed to hear, because as I said that whole week prior to the class he was tempted to go back to drinking.

Many shared that they would never again be rude to a drunk. That night, everyone in the class received a message from this man. It was the most profound Healing Circle I ever experienced. Everyone felt the same, and acknowledged they would never again judge a person by how they look, dress and act. Also he seemed comfortable with himself. He never apologized for who he was, how he looked and, most importantly, what we thought about him. What a lesson!

Everyone is here on the planet to have their own experience. It is his life and this is how our visitor chose to live it. What was most important was why we all attracted him that night. It was because we all had a strong desire to move past issues we were still stuck in and not fully aware of. We still had many negative thoughts and beliefs which were not serving us. That shadow side of ourselves is what we think we hide from others, but the shadow part will always rear its ugly head when we least expect it. This class was clear evidence of how unresolved emotions will continue to attract situations that are a match to how we have been thinking and feeling.

As it was confirmed that night, that for many of us meeting this gentleman outside the church, most of us would not have given this man a second glance. Yet on the surface all of us were intelligent, well dressed, and had a generally comfortable life. But why were some of us still being challenged by how we felt about ourselves? It is said "You teach what you need to learn." What I needed to learn at the time was about self-esteem, worthiness and forgiveness. And as like attracts like, many in the group had similar challenges. Yet I feel good about myself most of the time, but it's easy for me to lose some of that inner strength that I know I have, but do not always trust. My inner core was sometimes fragile and easily swayed. By this I mean it's easy for me to forget who I really am and my many accomplishments. This man came to remind us who we really were and to give us an opportunity to revisit our past unresolved issues if we were willing to see beyond our judgment around this messenger.

FORGIVENESS ALTAR: The Purpose For The Altar Is An Assigned Space Where You Can Place Items That Represent Things That You Want In Your Life. And, most importantly, this space is where you are honouring yourself.

Divide the altar into two sections. On the left side of the altar place items or names of people in your life you are having challenges with. Those people you need to forgive.

After you do the Forgiveness Visualization, transfer the names that you were willing to forgive to the right side.

You may repeat this visualization as many times as you wish and use it as a catalyst to free yourself and to move forward with your life.

Forgiveness Visualization

You may want to play some soothing music. Allow the music to relax you. Create a place for yourself (I call it my sanctuary) in your mind where you will feel calm, strong and confident. I like to use the image of a glass dome. The sun is streaming thought the glass windows. Some of the windows are stained glass. This throws beautiful colours around the room. I have my special comfortable lounge chair that I sit in. There are also brilliant crystals in the room. I have also placed flowers and foliage in my sanctuary.

Find a comfortable place to lie down. You may want to turn off the phone. Breathe in for the count of three. Hold the breath for the count of three and then exhale for the count of three. Repeat this breath two more times. Feel the body relaxing more and more. Now think only happy thoughts. Remember joyful experiences you had. Allow the feeling of those events to move easily through your body. If you remember something funny and you feel like laughing do so. Feel the appreciation you have for your life and remind yourself who you truly are, a loving, joyous being and an extension of your higher self.

Now imagine you are bringing one of the people you feel you want to forgive into your sanctuary. If you have reservations about how this person may react when you speak with them, you may want to imagine they are outside your sanctuary. Some may want to place them in another dome, but you can both see and hear each other clearly.

Before you speak with them allow yourself to remember good things about the relationship. Allow yourself to relive these events. If funny things happened allow yourself to chuckle to yourself. If the duration of the relationship was short, see if you can find something about them you can appreciate. It may be you like the way they wear their hair, or the colour of their eyes. There must be something you can find to appreciate. Be willing to find that thing or things.

Now imagine that you are speaking with them. You tell them that you realize that despite all the blame you have placed on them over the years, that you were a part of this manifestation. You acknowledge your beliefs, thoughts and feelings about yourself and/or them brought you together to co-create this event. You are now willing to set them free. You no longer harbour anger and resentment towards them. Watch, feel and listen for their reply. Do not expect that they will understand what you mean by your words. It does not matter as long as you truly believe that you mean what you are saying. Some may get angry and walk away. Others may speak and some may just be silent. It does not matter. What matters is you mean what you say. You are now ready to move past all the blame you held towards this person. You may not forget, but you are willing to get through it to move beyond the ordeal.

1) When you feel complete, thank them for coming.

2) You may want to take some time to journal you thoughts and feelings.

3) Before you bring the next person in take a few breaths in and out again.

4) Play soothing music if you wish.

5) Most importantly think happy thoughts so that you are feeling good before you speak to the next person.

6) Now bring in the next person, and continue to do the same thing with all of those you need to forgive.

7) You do not have to do them all in one sitting. You will know when to stop for the session.

8) Do not worry about those who have walked out on you since you have expressed how you feel and owned your part in all of this. Some people just want to remain miserable and angry. If this concerns you it is because you would like to leave the situation all neatly packaged. I would suggest you remember only the good parts of the relationship. This good part could mean that you thank them for coming into your life to show you where your thoughts were at the time of your encounter.

Do not forget to transfer the names or the objects that represent the people you forgave to the right side of the altar.

Those You Are Not Ready To Forgive:

1) Make a gratitude journal and in it make a list of something you can appreciate about them. It could be something as simple as the way they wear their hair, the colour of their eyes. If we want to find something positive we can.

2) If you cannot find anything positive to say write pages and pages on other things in your life you appreciate.

3) If you wish to heal this relationship, eventually ask the universe to give you guidance. "Universe, I would like to heal this relationship. Let us communicate at the perfect time and let the interaction be easy, light and comfortable and healing for us both."

4) When you feel ready you may want to write a letter to them. This letter does not have to be mailed to them.

5) You could write a letter to a friend (you do not have to mail it either) to let them know how well those relationships you had challenges with are doing.

6) Write a list of what you now want in your relationships. For example, "I want to have friends who are appreciators, talented, and creative. Some have liked different things, but we encourage our differences"

7) If you were not wiling to release anyone, turn your attention to other things in you life that make you feel good.

Once you feel you have released and let go, you now move the item or the name of the person to the other side of the altar. When you have released them all, you could burn or bury the items.

We did this exercise at a weekend workshop. One night we built a huge bonfire and each person released people in their lives they had challenges with and also aspects of themselves they no longer wanted to hold on to. It was a powerful experience.

One year when this workshop was held in Mexico, the altar was created at the start of the week. As the participants did their work they kept moving their items to the forgiveness side of the altar. Anyone that they could not come to a completion with, they continued to work with on their own with the exercises they learned in the class or through a private session.

On the final day everyone who wanted to share had an opportunity to share who or what situation they forgave. There was great celebration.

Then as a group we all walked down to the ocean and threw our items in the ocean. Most of the items were from the ocean like seashells, seaweed and some beautiful flowers. This was a magical moment, but you can create your own rituals of forgiveness.

Yourself

If you have placed yourself on the altar, use the same process as above.

1) Write yourself a letter, telling yourself how wonderful you are. Include all your new goals and the great relationships you are now enjoying. Mail the letter to yourself about two weeks after you did the exercise. This letter will serve as a reminder of the things you are now wanting in your life. You can continue this exercise with yourself for as long as you wish.

2) If you did the exercise in Chapter 2, you may want to re-read the appreciation notes and listen to the tape you made.

3) Once you feel you have released and let go, you can now move the name/object that represents the person or yourself, to the other side of the altar.

When you have released them all, burn or bury the items.

Now you are ready to start anew feeling less weighted down by others Now you have given yourself permission to move forward.

Setting New Goals For Yourself.

1) Make a list of all the things you now want in your life. For example:

   What you now want about relationships
   What you now want about money
   What you now want about you work
   What you now want about your health
   And anything else you have been desiring

2) Observe your thoughts and feelings especially about the things you want. Become more conscious about what you are focusing on.

3) Spend time visualizing yourself the way you want your life to be now. Do the visualization because it feels good to imagine your new life. Include all of your senses. Expect that what you want is on its way to you and watch for evidence from the source.

Once I was waiting at the airport while my husband was in line to pick up our rental car. Next to me sat a lady, and as I glanced over to her I noticed she had the tiniest pocketbook. In the book were pictures of the things she wanted. I knew this because I have been doing this since my real estate days. The only difference is I have my goals on boards in my office where I can see them. So here was this lady enjoying her dream while her children quietly played. Most of us would more than likely be upset, because the line was so long and things were moving slowly.

The Altar As Sacred Space

Once you have completed your "GOALS LIST" find objects that represent some of these things you want. The items can be anything from a pencil, crystals, rings, candles, flowers, pictures, words, angels, stuffed animals. But they all represent something that you want.

1) The first thing to place on the altar is a picture of yourself. It could be a baby picture or one of you at any age. The most important part is that you like the picture. If you do not have one that you really like about you, choose the one you like the most from what you have. Place this one on the altar until you get the one you really like. This is the first part of the exercise and the most important part. Remember I said this place is about your honouring you.

   Whenever this instruction is given to my students some of them will have a lot of resistance to placing a picture of themselves on display. Many feel it is boasting, but once it is discussed we discover it is about them not loving themselves.

   I had one student who came up with all kinds of reasons as to why she could not do the altar. Her final resistance was that she had no place in her room. Her mother, who was in the class at the same time, said this was not the case. There was ample space to place this alter. A student in the class even offered to come over and help her to set it up. She also refused this offer. I share this with you so that you can notice how you are feeling about doing this exercise.

Are you happy to do it or do you have resistance to it? Many feel vain. We are not used to honouring ourselves. This exercise is about honouring SELF. We need to place ourselves first above all else. And for many of us the reason for not wanting to forgive is because over the years we have placed others ahead of our needs. By not valuing our lives we have become resentful and angry towards those who value theirs, or who we feel took advantage of us.

So the placement of the altar is a way for us to take back our power. Not to have power over others but to feel more empowered about our lives.

2) An angel could represent for you the loving unconditional heart you want to have. If you write many contracts (such as Real Estate) you may want to place a special pen to mean "All my successful contracts." A word like "abundance" could also mean unlimited prosperity to you. A stuffed toy could represent that happy, loving, tender relationship. You can choose anything, as long as you give it meaning.

   This can be so much fun and you will find that you will continue to add and replace new items as you start manifesting the things that you l

3) The altar can be as large or as small as you wish. Many of my clients have altars on their office desk. No one knows because it does not look like a sacred space. They generally place items that conform to office protocol. They may have a special pen, a paper clip, and a penny to which they have given these items meaning. What some have noticed is that when they created the altar that the employers they interact with will come into their office and say "I do not know why I have come into your office." They are being drawn to the energy that the person created around this space.

I had two ladies who came to the class from quite a distance. They stayed in a hotel overnight for two-day workshop. One afternoon they spent some time looking for objects to create their individual altars. Keep in mind they were in a hotel. They used simple things from nature to represent the things they wanted for now until they went home and recreated their scared space. They had strong desire after releasing their past and realizing that they, and only they, were responsible for what was going on in their lives.

Hallie's Story

One of my students, Hallie, has hives. She felt guilt because she did not know how to say no to people who placed demands on her. This resulted in her feeling angry, guilty and depressed. For as far back as she could remember she was always taking care of other people. She was tired of cooking and cleaning for all of the family gatherings, like Christmas, Thanksgiving and birthday parties. She reached the point in her life where she decided that she did not want to be the one responsible for these main events, or even the daily household chores she has been responsible for the past 50 years. In addition, her sister who had been her rival since childhood had been ill for a long time. Hallie spent long hours looking after her. Now Hallie has decided that she no longer wants to assist her sister. Now her challenge is that she was having trouble feeling good when she says no to these people. She feels guilty and feels she is very selfish to not want to help them, mostly because she does not work for her living.

Hallie has had fewer attacks of hives, but the times they are at their worst are when she is stressed or feeling guilt and angry after saying no. She shared with me that she is becoming clearer and clearer about not wanting to feel responsible for all these people anymore. She has been ill for the past three weeks, staying home because the hives have appeared in visible areas on her body. She has also realized that as a child her relationship with her sister was never healthy. Apparently she was always jealous of her sister because her sister was the favoured one. All of the processing around her feelings and emotions resulted in new, full-blown hives. Now, she justifies not helping these people because she is ill. Fortunately for Hallie she understands what her hives are about. But many people are creating dis-ease in their bodies and do not make the connection that the illness is related to how they are thinking and feeling.

Some suggestions Hallie received:

1) Find something about these people to appreciate.

2) Only offer to do for them if this is what she wanted, meaning when she offered it would be because she feels good about assisting them.

3) See herself in the future enjoying her life, doing things that make her feel good.

Student's comments

"Since working with these principles and tools, my life has been transformed. I now realize that my joy is the most important thing in my life. I feel like a weight has been lifted from my body and my heart. I have so much more energy. And I find I am laughing, singing, dancing and exploring and trusting more. All aspects of my life and all my relationships have been enriched and enhanced. I have manifested a car and many other wonderful things. I now have a more full, loving heart and a more joyful life. Thank you Marlene, for your guidance." M.C.

"I have asked the universe for the family to be cared for and healed. I have received 2 letters from the brother, with the blessings of the mother, to write to me in effect to understand how and why I took his sister's life. I am in the process of establishing meaningful contact through the mediator to help him understand why I did what I did." D.D.

Synopsis

Only we know if we need to forgive ourselves and/or someone else in our life. We get to choose. The situations and people in our life that we are attracting and interacting with will be our gauge. The people in our life that we are having challenges with will mirror back to us where we are on the journey. These are the ones, the ones we gave so much power and energy to, we more than likely need to forget. We no longer hold our grudges and are willing to own our past in the attracting of the event. As a result: OUR LIVES CAN BECOME THE WAY WE HAVE DREAMED AND IMAGINED THEM TO BE. They are a gift to help us move forward and become the true lovers that we came here to be.

For the next few days practice appreciation and focus upon whatever makes you feel good so that you can start to see the evidence of these steps working for you.

You will start to thrive and the universal powers will yield to you all of what you have been wanting.

chapter Seven

Health
How the body gets our attention through pain

Joyous Living Skill #7: Tell Your Body What You Want In The Positive, And Your Body Will Oblige.

One of my clients, Earl, illustrates the body/mind connection when he was treated for a slipped disk caused by a childhood fall from a tree. After 25 years of emotional fatigue, he went to a chiropractor who told him he was "out of alignment." We, too, are "out of alignment" with our Higher Self when we experience emotional, spiritual or physical dis-ease. By focusing on our problems, we draw attention to the very thing we wish to be rid of. The pain is an indication of how far we are from the source of our healing. From now on consider your pain as a point of power, an indication it's time to alter your thinking and feeling about your physical problem in order to solve it. By reconnecting with your source, you are able to bring healing spiritual energy to the physical manifestation.

In Earl's own words: "I realized my pain was directly linked to my physical and emotional vibration. My disconnection from Source energy that had the power to heal and rejuvenate my spirit, soul, mind and body left me restless, anxious, fearful and in pain. I have discovered that my strongly focused desire for Source energy to heal my body has been the purest medicine to be healthy and active.

While meditating in the prison chapel I found myself imaging a peaceful institutional transfer from medium to minimum security. I imaged a lower security prison environment while walking in the more relaxed atmosphere. During these moments of envisioning peace, harmony, and freedom from incarceration the pain in my back and leg was alleviated. As I walked out of the chapel to return to my cell I thought only of being free. I felt light on my feet and pain free for the first time in eleven months. As I rounded the corner of the building and proceeded to my living unit another prisoner commented that I seemed to be walking better. I replied that I felt good. What we call to mind is often what becomes manifest in our lives, drawing to ourselves the wants, desires and needs that we think of in our daily lives. Through this we will discover harmony, balance and well-being.

By allowing myself to think positive thoughts for improved health my physical disposition became greatly improved as a result of my realignment to the positive emotional vibration I radiated to my lower back and sciatic nerve. Being in the flow of Source energy has been a pain-free experience. Now, I continue to image the clearing of osteoarthritis from my spine so that I can enter my senior years, pain free." E.F.

Pick up any newspaper, or turn on your television and you can easily become overwhelmed with disease and medical ways of curing it. If the common cold wasn't bad enough, now we have a vaccine resistant flu, which can kill you. Not to mention the terrorists ready to unleash biochemical weapons on the unsuspecting populations of the world. What about the ozone layer? And if that's not enough, have you been on an airplane lately? It takes longer to get through security than to get to your destination once you are on the plane. The new millennium has brought us new drugs and treatments which barely keep up with the new dis-eases and conditions plaguing modern society. About the only thing medical science can agree on is that emotional health is connected to our physical well being. Something that eastern medicine has known since before the last millennium.

If we can accept the connection between our emotional health and our physical well-being, then it makes sense to prevent dis-ease where it starts, with our emotional body. Feelings are powerful. Medical science has proven that depression causes change at the cellular level, which is why it is so important to treat it as soon as it is diagnosed. If it is a chemical imbalance, then it is important to restore the balance to alleviate the depression. Feeling good is the best antidote for emotional or physical dis-ease. Your body will tell you what hurts. Not just the obvious pain of a sprain, or a torn muscle, but the emotional pain of years of negative self-talk or external abuse. Eastern medicine is based on analyzing the body and its language in order to establish a dialog with the mind and spirit. Once the channels of communication are open between the three elements of human beings, balance is restored and with balance comes health and well-being.

Exercise

To demonstrate where you hold tension in your body, allow yourself to go fully into the experience.

Take a moment now, close your eyes and allow yourself to think of something, someone, or a situation that makes you feel angry, depressed or any negative emotion you are familiar with. Allow yourself to go fully into the experience and feelings. Notice what the body does as you recall this incident. For some people, their jaw tightens, some feel knots in the stomach, and some feel the tension in the head and shoulders. Some say they feel a headache starting. Now take in a nice full long breath and exhale. Let go of all those negative feelings. Blow them out with the exhale

Now think of something, someone or an event that pleases you. Go fully into the feelings and the situation. Now notice what the body does, how it softens, relaxes. Some say it feels like the body expands and the mind feels more peaceful.

Open your eyes. This simple exercise shows us how our body follows our mind.

In the days that follow, keep a mental chart or write down how your body reacts to stress, emotional situations or conflict. Also, note how your body reacts to the wonderful things that happen during the day.

Eastern medicine has defined areas in our bodies which communicate physically how we are emotionally and spiritually. These energy centers, or chakras, represent a spiritual life lesson we must learn in order to progress down our path. When we are feeling good, accepting ourselves and others, the energy flows freely throughout our body. However, whenever we are challenged by a life lesson, that challenge can be felt in the individual chakra which is associated with that aspect of the material world.

Carolyn Myss, in her book Anatomy Of The Spirit, presents the chakra as individual spiritual lessons each individual must learn. "As a person masters each chakra, he gains power and self-knowledge that become integrated into his spirit advancing him along the path towards spiritual consciousness in the classic hero's

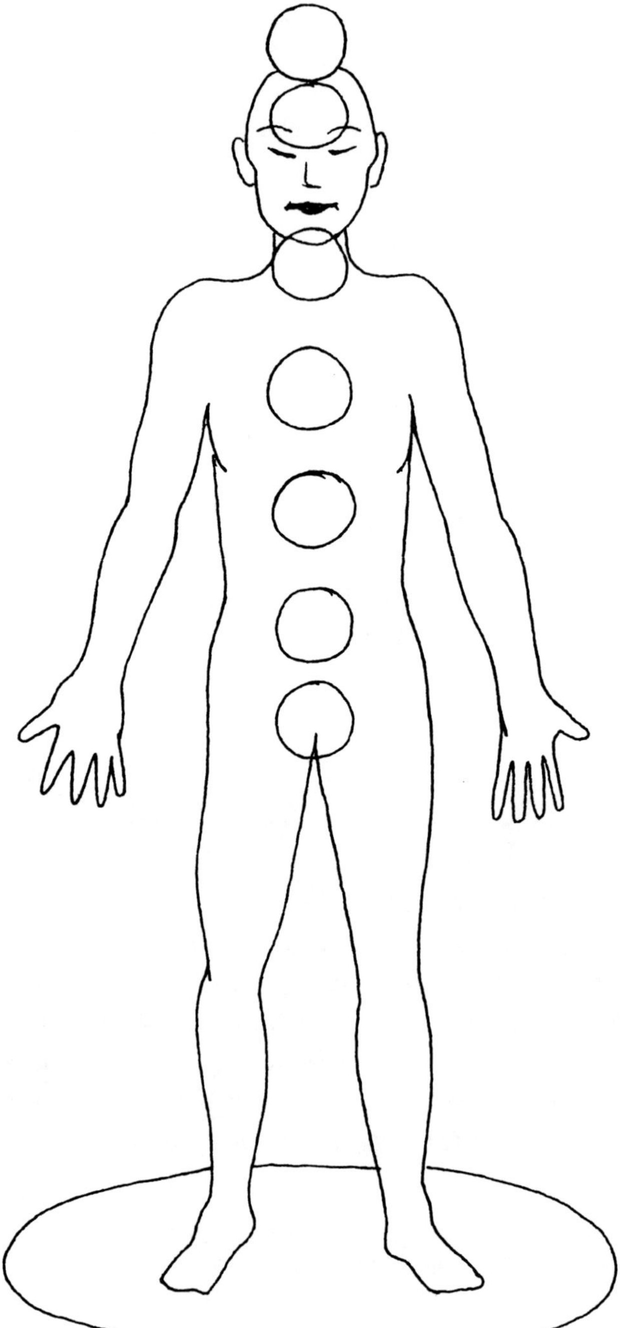

journey." (Myss, Caroline, *Anatomy Of The Spirit*, Harmony Books, New York, 1996, page 68) Whether you view them as internal signals to your emotional well being, or indicators of your physical well-being, your spiritual health will be enhanced by a thorough understanding of them.

There are seven body chakras. The parts of the body with which they are associated communicate different emotional patterns.

Exercise

Draw a simple outline of the human body.

At the top of the head, write 7th—CROWN

At the point between the eyebrows, write 6th—THIRD EYE

At the throat, write 5th—THROAT

At the chest, write 4th— HEART

At the base of the ribs, write 3rd—SOLAR PLEXUS

Below the navel, write 2nd—SACRAL

At the pubic bone, write 1st—BASE

On the left hand side of the page, list 1-7

1) BASE CHAKRA—CONSCIOUSNESS—JUDGMENT
2) SACRAL CHAKRA—FEAR AND ANXIETY
3) SOLAR PLEXUS CHAKRA—FEELING POWERLESS
4) HEART CHAKRA—LOVE FELT FOR SELF
5) THROAT CHAKRA—LOVE EXPRESSED
6) THIRD EYE CHAKRA—SEEING THE CREATION IN ALL THINGS
7) CROWN CHAKRA----------------SEAT OF NO JUDGMENT

As you read the following descriptions, you may identify with one or more chakra experiences.

1) The Base - Judgment Chakra

This chakra is located below the hips. Feelings of judgment of self are located on this area. It manifests itself in the hips, knees, legs and the feet, such as joint problems and arthritis.

Harriet's Story

Harriet's mother died when she was only eight years of age. She had two brothers who were younger than herself. Her father did not deal well with her mother's death. As a way to deny his feelings, he worked long hours and many times did not return home until they were all asleep. He spent very little time with them and he brought in many different baby-sitters to watch over them. Harriet felt sorry for her little brothers. They missed their mother and many times begged their father to come home to be with them. She did everything she could to make them happy and keep them comfortable. When she grew older she helped them with their homework, fixed their lunches and even tried to cook some meals and bake them cookies.

This continued until the boys left home and Harriet was finally able to start dating. She eventually married, not so much because she loved this man, but rather she saw him as an opportunity to marry someone who was wealthy who would take care of her.

This was not the case as her husband was a workaholic and he, too, was seldom at home. They had three children she reared on her own because of his busy work schedule. She started to judge herself, thinking that maybe she was not a good wife. If she tried harder to please her husband she thought he would spend more time with her. Harriet started to have knee problems. Eventually she had to support herself with a walking stick. Harriet's continuous negative judgment of herself had created the arthritis in her knees. She needed to stop judging herself and others.

2) Sacral Chakra - Fear and Anxiety

The second chakra is located in the area below the belly button. Feelings of fear and anxiety are located here. Pain manifests as any gas, or indigestion below the navel.

Catherine's Story

Catherine and her brother were twins. Right after they were born their parents left them with a baby-sitter for months at a time. Their parents both traveled for their individual companies and they both would be out of the city (and in some cases the country) for months. As Catherine grew older she would have many sleepless nights waiting and hoping that one or both of the parents would come home to them. She remembers always feeling fearful and anxious. The sitters treated them well and Catherine and her brother clung to the sitters, fearing that they, too, might one day leave them!

She eventually married, but even though her husband was very understanding and attentive, Catherine always had a fear that he, too, would one day leave her.

She developed bladder problems. Everywhere she went she carried some form of protection, just in case she could not control her bladder. This would happen mostly when she felt fearful and anxious. To heal this challenge, Catherine needed to start trusting herself and others more.

3) Solar Plexus Chakra - Power

The third chakra is located just above the navel at the base of the rib. Feelings of powerlessness are located here. Pain manifests just above the navel as ulcers, gallbladder and liver problems.

Nancy's Story

Nancy felt smothered by her mother. Her mother lived her life to take care of her and her older brother. There was a lot of tension between her mother and father. Her mother never worked and her father, on the other hand, had a job that demanded a lot of after-work business/social meetings. Her mother did her best to compensate for her father's absence. Many times her mother would join her father in these meetings.

Her brother, who was much older, spent most of his time out with his friends.

Nancy felt alone and abandoned. She spent many of her meals either eating by herself or with her mother. She hated eating her meals with her mother because she insisted that Nancy eat everything on her plate. As a form of rebelling towards both parents, Nancy started to create many ways not to be present at mealtimes. She felt like her life was spinning out of control. She starved herself and it soon developed into bulimia. Nancy felt that her body was the only thing in her life over which she had control.

4) Heart Chakra - Love Felt for Self

The fourth chakra is located at the heart. Feelings of lack of love for self are located here. Pain manifests from the solar plexus to the base of the neck as heart attacks, hypertension, anxiety and breathing difficulties in the lungs.

Ned's Story

Ned always placed other people's needs before his own. This gave him a lot of satisfaction. It made him feel needed and appreciated. He grew up in a large family. His parents always preached lack and shortage There was never enough. None of the children received any special attention. He grew up feeling that he was not deserving of nice things. Since he never felt love from his parents, Ned grew up not knowing how to love himself. Ned learned to bury his feelings. He did not like to talk about how he felt, no matter how depressed he was. He had difficulty telling other that he loved them and, in turn, he did not feel deserving of love.

This all finally escalated into pains in his chest, which the doctors diagnosed as angina. Ned needed to start loving himself more and he needed to speak more positively about himself.

5) Throat Chakra - Love Expressed

The fifth chakra is located at the throat. Feelings of lack of love expressed to others are located here. Pain manifests as sinus problems, breathing difficulties and throat infections.

Martin's Story

Martin placed high standards on himself. He was a pleaser, so he allowed many people to take advantage of him. He allowed his friends and family to place unreasonable demands on him. He had a difficult time saying no to them, and started to feel burdened with everyone's demands. He internalized all his angry feelings towards them. He had constant pain in his shoulders. He developed many cold, sinus and throat infections. He was very unhappy about the responsibilities that he allowed his family to place on him. He felt tremendous guilt when he said no to them. Martin needed to learn how to say no to the things that did not please him. He also had to learn not to feel guilty when he says no.

6) Third Eye Chakra - Seeing the Creator in all things

The sixth chakra is located in the area of the eyes and ears. Feelings of lack of appreciation for all things are located here. Pain will manifest as sinus problems, asthma and allergies.

Betty's Story

Betty suffered from constant allergies. She continually complained about her relationship and the challenges she had with her children. Nothing they did pleased her. She always seemed to find fault with what they did. She resisted change, argued her point and insisted that she was right. Her insistence on her opinions and her refusal to listen to others' suggestions resulted in her challenges with her allergies. She could not appreciate the value of differing opinions that others brought to her relationships. She needs to be willing to accept that everyone's opinions have value.

7) Crown Chakra - Seat of No Judgment

The seventh chakra is called the Crown. Feelings of judgment of self and others are located here. Pain will manifest in the forehead and the top of the head as headaches and migraines.

Holly's Story

Holly held a very responsible job. She loved her work, but she had many challenges with her boss and some of the employees. She worried constantly about her performance and the performance of those around her. These concerns left her feeling drained and agitated by the end of the day. She had many sleepless nights worrying about the next day. Often, by the time she arrived at work she had already developed a headache, which soon escalated into a migraine headache. Some days the pain was so intense she had to leave. Her many absent days from work resulted in her being fired from her job.

Holly has to learn to appreciate others more.

Involvement With More Than One Chakra

My Story: Anorexia

When I was 16, I developed anorexia. My oldest sister was very outgoing and loved sports. These activities helped her bond more with my father who also loved sports. I felt at times that my father did not love me. I know now that this was not the case, but as a child this was my perception. My younger sister had her own friends and kept to herself. I was the one at home, and my outlet was my dance classes. I was very shy, insecure, had low self-esteem and clearly did not love myself. I was only five feet tall and pleasantly plump. My sisters used to tease me. I was very sensitive and would cry easily. I did not like what they did, so I decided one day I would show them that I could slim down. I lost weight and everyone was saying how good I looked. This made me feel better about myself, and it eased the insecurity I felt at times.

The weight loss got out of control, because I became addicted with looking good and the compliments of others. I went from 110 to 85 pounds. I would starve myself for days. I eventually moved out of my parents' house to marry. I believe that my marriage turned my life around.

The chakras involved here were the second chakra (not loving self), the third chakra (feeling powerless), and the first chakra (judgment).

Tammy's Story

Tammy was the firstborn in a culture that does not hold women in high regard. The men are favoured, and women are considered second-class citizens. Tammy's brother was the second child in the family. Tammy was highly intelligent, holding many degrees including a Ph.D. She was one of the pioneers with the computers, and she traveled around the world due to her expertise. Apparently, no matter how intelligent and successful she was, it was never good enough for her father. The son was the apple of the father's eye and was highly praised. This treatment led her to believe that she was not good enough, not worthy, and that she was not loved. She realized that, no matter how well she did it was never good enough in daddy's eyes. She felt powerless in the situation.

When I met her she was in the hospital with cancer. She was in an unhappy marriage, and had a daughter in her early teens. She had lost all her hair due to the radiation therapy. Her parents would visit from their country and dad would sit in the room without saying a word to his daughter. He did not even acknowledge her.

I pointed out to her one time, "Can't you see? Now you even look like a boy (losing all the hair), and he still does not notice you."

All of her striving as a young woman to prove to her father that she was good enough, or as worthy as her brother, was in vain. In both of these examples, the fourth chakra (not loving self), the first chakra (judgment) and the third chakra (feeling powerless) were involved.

These examples illustrate the power of the mind over the body. Negativity will manifest pain and dis-ease in specific parts of the body. Depending on the symptoms, we can locate the source of the pain. Keeping in mind that modern medicine is here to help us through intervention and treatment, we can still aid the process by paying attention to what may have caused the pain in the first place. In understanding the chakras, and the source of our dis-ease, we can strive to prevent further occurrences by changing our thoughts and feelings.

Skills to Creating Greater Physical Well-Being

Chakra Invocations

What is an invocation?

Literally translated from Latin an invocation is "a calling within." It is an outward expression of an inner desire. Just by expressing the desire, we are suggesting to the universe that we are expecting the outcome. If we add positive feelings to the invocation, the universe responds in a positive way by giving you what you asked for when it comes to your health.

The following are the invocations for each body chakra. As you utter these affirmations, imagine and envision a healing light and the departure of pain from each area:

You may use any of these opening statements:

- from the lord god of my being,
- from the light within,
- from all that I am,
- from the goddess within,
- from the bottom of my heart,

or any statement you may want to create.

1) BASE - JUDGMENT

(Pain manifests here as discomfort in the hips, knees and/ or thighs.)

FROM THE LORD GOD OF MY BEING, I NOW GIVE MYSELF PERMISSION TO STOP JUDGING MYSELF...SO BE IT...(Inhale and exhale 3 times).

2) SACRAL CHAKRA - FEAR AND ANXIETY

(Pain manifests here as any gas or indigestion below the navel.)

FROM THE LORD GOD OF MY BEING, I NOW GIVE MYSELF PERMISSION TO FEEL MY FEARS, TO SEE, TO KNOW AND TO UNDERSTAND WHAT THESE FEARS ARE ABOUT. I ALSO GIVE MYSELF PERMISSION TO EXPERIENCE THEM IN A LOVING, PEACEFUL, PAINLESS, JOYOUS WAY...SO BE IT... (Inhale and exhale 3 times).

3) SOLAR PLEXUS CHAKRA - POWER

(Pain manifests just above the navel.)

FROM THE LORD GOD OF MY BEING, I NOW GIVE MYSELF PERMISSION TO TAKE BACK MY POWER FROM ANY MAN, WOMAN OR CHILD FROM MY PAST LIVES, FROM THIS LIFETIME AND FROM THIS DAY FORWARD. I RELEASE MYSELF...SO BE IT...(Inhale and exhale 3 times).

4) HEART CHAKRA - LOVE FELT FOR SELF

(Pain manifests from the solar plexus to the base of the neck.)

FROM THE LORD GOD OF MY BEING, I NOW GIVE MYSELF PERMISSION TO LOVE MYSELF, AND TO SAY THAT I AM WORTHY AND DESERVING. I DESERVE TO BE ON THIS PLANET AND FROM THIS DAY FORWARD I WILL INVITE INTO MY LIFE PEOPLE WHO WILL LOVE ME JUST THE WAY I AM ...SO BE IT...(Inhale and exhale 3 times).

5) THROAT CHAKRA - LOVE EXPRESSED

(Pain manifests from the bridge of the nose to the chin.)

FROM THE LORD GOD OF MY BEING, I NOW GIVE MYSELF PERMISSION TO SAY THAT I AM NO LONGER RESPONSIBLE FOR PEOPLE IN MY LIFE WHO DO NOT BRING ME JOY..SO BE IT...(Inhale and exhale 3 times).

6) EYES & EARS CHAKRA - SEEING THE CREATOR IN ALL THINGS

(Pain manifests in the bridge of the nose to middle of the forehead.)

FROM THE LORD GOD OF MY BEING, I NOW GIVE MYSELF PERMISSION TO SEE GOD IN ALL...SO BE IT...(Inhale and exhale 3 times).

7) CROWN CHAKRA - SEAT OF NO JUDGMENT

(Pain manifests in the middle of the forehead to the top of the head.)

FROM THE LORD GOD OF MY BEING, I NOW GIVE MYSELF PERMISSION TO SEE THE PERFECTION IN THE MOMENT...SO BE IT...(Inhale and exhale 3 times).

Try these affirmations each day as you quiet your mind and breathe for relaxation and release.

Timothy's Story:

Client Uses Tools To Change

Timothy is a 46-year-old executive, who is married, but divorced once His fear of never being good enough drives him personally and professionally. Because of his need to show others that he is worthy, he feels lonely, guilt- ridden and powerless. Eventually, after a period of deteriorating health, his doctor told him he had prostrate cancer. Timothy knew he needed to change his feelings about himself in order to heal his own body. Intuitively, he understood that his unhappiness manifested itself in his physical symptoms. He took back control of his life and made some changes to heal.

Rather than focus upon his disease, he shifted his focus to appreciation of his body. He concentrated his conversation on any other topic that made him feel good. He listened to his doctor's advice. Instead of these visits creating anxiety, he viewed them as a solution to this dis-ease. Timothy wrote happy, positive stories about himself and his family in the future. Timothy appreciated his family and friends, his natural surroundings, beautiful sounds and even his illness for bringing him to this new understanding.

An energized and contented Timothy used many skills in order to take control and better his health. Some of them are listed below.

1) He wrote a story pretending five years had gone by, and what a wonderful life he is living. By writing a long letter to a friend with no mention of his past illness, and just focusing on all the wonderful things he and his family are enjoying now, Timothy experienced the joy of his future

2) He also appreciated his body by writing down everything about his body he liked.

3) He only focused on the good things about his body. If it was only one thing about his body he appreciated and focused on, the body will follow the mind.

4) He also did a lot of appreciating about other things he liked in life.

5) Before he fell asleep at night he told his body to relax and heal and rejuvenate itself. He wanted to wake up refreshed and energized.

6) He remembered the times when his body was healthy.

Apply these skills in your own life. For instance, write down positive things about your body, and other things about yourself in your life that you appreciate, and then carry it around with you. When you feel the pain, simply read what you have written down. Before long you are back to feeling good again.

This can also be done on a tape. I suggest you do the tape exercise at least two or three times. The first time you do it, you will discover that when you listen to the tape your voice does not sound in alignment with the words. But when you do it again you will notice a difference in the tone and you will know by the sound of your voice that you are feeling more in alignment with what you are asking for. Also, take your attention off your health challenge, and focus on anything else that makes you feels good. Stay happy and the body will follow. If you do these exercises for 30 days then you will see an improvement in your health.

Positive Visualization:

How You Inflict Physical And Emotional Pain On The Body.

Find a place that is comfortable and safe for you to do the exercise Take a few breaths in and out. On the exhalation feel the body relaxing and releasing more and more. Relax the large muscles in the stomach and the buttocks, hips and thighs. Continue to breathe gently until you feel completely relaxed and peaceful.

Now imagine yourself going through your day. Notice your recent thoughts and how you have been feeling. Have you been judging yourself or others? Are you having feelings of frustration around them, and maybe wanting them to do things your way? Do you believe that your way is the right way, and their way is the wrong? As you allow yourself to recall and observe these situations, notice your thoughts and feelings. Are your thoughts about these situations and people positive or negative? Notice how the body feels when you are interacting with these people in a negative way. And if the interaction is positive also notice how the body feels. Have you been feeling more unusual pain and tension in your body lately? Listen to your words as you interact with these people who challenge you. Maybe it is your mother, father, sisters, brothers, employer, employee or mate. Notice how much energy it takes to get them to listen to you and do what you would like them to do. Observe yourself giving them advice, and how they repeatedly have no intention of heeding your words. Notice how much this frustrates you because you feel that they are wrong, and at fault.

Notice the tension in your body as you think and see yourself interacting with them. Also notice how they react as you try to give them advice, and try to change them. You may be busy trying to get your point across In these times you may be so involved with trying to fix them that you do not observe how they may be feeling. You do not see their pain and anguish. Now that you have allowed yourself to see their reactions to you, see yourself now being willing to allow them to be who they are. No need to try and change them. Feel your acceptance of them. As you are allowing others to be who they are, notice how your body starts to feel. Now that you are no longer worrying about them, feel how the body starts to respond to your thoughts. Your thoughts of acceptance, love and understanding will allow you to let go of the role of caretaker and adviser. Feel how the body is responding to your letting go of your resistance to their behaviour.

Now that you will not be spending so much time worrying about them, what will you do with all this free time and energy you now have? Allow yourself to imagine how you will be using all these minutes, hours and days on yourself to fulfill some of the dreams you have for yourself. Notice how the body responds as you start to allow these images to unfold and present themselves. Feel or imagine renewed energy streaming into the body Notice how much lighter and freer the body feels. Maybe the pain that you had before this exercise seems to have melted away.

You may tell yourself that you will no longer abandon you because you are important too. Your release does not mean you do not love them, but that your need to love yourself must be first. When you are happy, you can help others be happy. You realize now that by being frustrated and angry with them, you were judging them. This does not make them happy and does not help them. You now realize that this caretaking and trying to fix people (who may not want to change) has not brought you joy because your dreams and desires were placed on hold. If you have any guilty thoughts about abandoning them, know that they will be fine, and that they will find their way in their own life journey.

Allow yourself to release them more and more. See them five years from now living happy, healthy, successful lives. Feel the freedom as you see yourself doing what you want to do more and more. Note how light the body feels, as there is much less tension in the neck and shoulders. The head feels light and the rest of the body is totally relaxed and pain-free

See yourself getting on with new things in life, like meeting new friends and being happy. It feels good to focus on your own happiness, because those you used to worry about are getting on with their lives.

Notice how good the body is feeling. How the mind is now filled with all kinds of happy excited ideas and images. You cannot wait to write down or draw some of these images and information. You feel ready now to implement some of these new ideas. You feel a sense of peace yet you are so energized and very focused.

You may want to make a promise to yourself tonight, that you will stay focused on you because you are important. Breathe in all that energy you have shared with others. Breathe it back into you. With each inhalation renew your body and with each exhalation release them more and more.

See yourself walking through the day with so much more energy. You have a ne sense of purpose for who you now are in the universe. This new you feels so good! Notice how you interact with people, just letting them be who they are. Feel how your body responds, and how good it is to feel no judgment towards them. You may want to thank those people for teaching you this powerful lesson. You now realize that you do not need to be caretaker to others. You are to love yourself and live your dreams. Let go of any more tension and feel the excitement inside of you as you start to live your life in a more joyful happy way.

Slowly coming back, bring all those feelings of excitement to fulfill your vision.

Exercises

1) You may want to journal your experience.
2) You may want to draw the vision of the new self you saw.
3) You may want to write more empowering affirmations to yourself.
4) You may want to write any new ideas and goals that came to your mind.
5) You may want to write letters of appreciation to people (you do not have to give it to them).

Visualization: The Power Of The Healing Colour.

Imagine yourself leaning up against a tree. As you are leaning, feel the strength of that tree trunk. Allow your body to be fully supported by this tree. Listen to the sounds of nature. There may be the sounds of a light breeze or the sound of children's voices in the distance. You are feeling more and more relaxed as you feel the sun on your face. The earth is draining all the tension from your body.

Take a few breaths in and out while you let go of your tension more and more. You begin to feel much more alert and in charge. Listen to the sounds of running water. You know there must be a river close by. Envision yourself as you begin to walk down the hill towards the sound of the running stream. As you approach the river, you notice that there is a raft at the edge of the water. Step into the raft and allow the current of the water to take you down the river. Make yourself comfortable. Lie down or sit and just allow the stream to carry you, as you begin to feel more and more relaxed.

As you float down the river, notice the beautiful red flowers on either sides of the riverbank. Allow the beautiful red colours to wash all over you. Take in the fragrance of these roses, carnations and other wild red coloured flowers, while the raft continues to carry you down this river. Continue to take in as much of the colours as you think your body needs.

As you continue down the river, you notice that on either side of the riverbanks are beautiful orange flowers, larkspurs, poppies, and other orange wildflowers. Again allow this orange colour to wash all over you. Take in as much of the brilliant orange as you feel. Smell the wonderful fragrance of these flowers. Absorb as much as you need while you are feeling more and more relaxed.

The raft continues down the river and you are feeling very relaxed but alert. You are now approaching the yellow flowers, daisies, buttercups, roses, carnations, sunflowers. Smell the essence of these flowers. Allow the colour to wash all over your body, taking in as much of that colour as you need.

The raft continues to support you as you feel more and more relaxed and revitalized. Now you are approaching beautiful pink flowers and lush green foliage. There are peonies, carnations, and roses on either side of the riverbank. Allow that healing colour to wash over you now. Take in the smell of these beautiful flowers as the raft moves down the river.

You are now approaching the breath taking blue flowers such as morning glories, irises, and bluebells. There are several different shades of blue. Breathe in the essence of theses wonderful flowers as you allow this colour to wash all over you. Soak in as much as you feel your body needs.

Every cell in your body is revitalizing itself as you approach and start moving through the beautiful indigo flowers. There are rows and rows of violets. Breathe in this colour while your body absorbs what it needs You are feeling more and more alert and energized.

The raft continues down the river. On either side are beautiful white flowers including roses, carnations, and daisies. They are breath taking Allow this colour to wash all over you. Take in as much of this colour as you need. Breathe in the different smells that these plants are offering you.

You are coming to the end of the journey as the raft rests against the bank of the river. You notice that some being is waiting to welcome you You step off the raft and you greet the being. You realize that this is your inner being. Your inner being now guides you through a beautiful garden, and you find a place to sit and be comfortable. Your inner being invites you to ask any question you may have. Take as much time as you need to ask your questions.

You are coming to the end of your visit. You thank your higher self for this opportunity to visit your inner being who now leads you back through the garden to the raft. Your inner being says "I am always available to answer your questions; all you need to do is ask." You make a promise to yourself that you will take more time to visit and ask questions. You say your goodbyes. Just before you step onto the raft, your inner being gives you a gift. Accept the offering. It could be a word, a symbol, or object. You step back onto the raft and the river begins to once more support you back to your original starting point. As you continue through the different flower banks, you allow the colours to wash over you if you feel this is what your body requires.

The raft moves through the white flowers. It starts to approach the indigo flowers, continuing on, moving towards the blue flowers, carrying you to and passing through the pink flowers and green foliage. You continue to absorb as much of these colours and breathe in the fragrance of these beautiful flowers. You approach the yellow flowers, passing through these magnificent colours, while the raft carries you back to your destination. Every cell in your body is now vibrating with these brilliant colours You are now passing through the orange flowers. You are feeling wise, clear and more energized. The raft approaches the red flowers, moving calmly through the red as it starts to come back to its starting place and rest along the bank of the river.

You step off the raft and walk back up the hill to the tree where you originally started this meditation. You sit and lean against the tree as you think back to your experience.

Allow yourself to become fully present when you feel ready to do so.

Exercises

1) You may want to draw the images you saw.

2) You may want to write down your experience with your inner being.

3) In the days to come take note because some of what you asked your inner being for may come to pass.

4) You may see evidence of the gift you received. One of my clients when she did this meditation received a flower from her inner being. Two days later someone sent her a bouquet of flowers.

5) If you do not receive a simple gift such as flowers then you may want to buy yourself a flower, or if you have flowers in a garden, cut yourself a few.

6) If you received a gift and you did not open it, here are two (of many) possible reasons: you could be afraid to see what was inside or you do not feel worthy of receiving gifts. You may want to ask your source to inspire you to open the gift at the perfect time. State that when you do finally open the gift it will be a loving, joyful and uplifting experience. When the inspiration comes, find a safe, quiet and comfortable place. Imagine yourself receiving the gift from your inner being. When you feel ready, open the gift. You could see yourself sitting under the tree, or on the raft. You choose which feels best for you. You will be so delighted with the gift, and wonder why you did not open the gift sooner.

7) If you cannot go and open the gift you may want to go out and buy yourself a small gift. (This does not have to be expensive, but something you would like to have.) Get the salesperson to gift-wrap the present. Then when you unwrap this gift, appreciate yourself, and remember how much you enjoyed buying yourself this present.

8) You may want to journal your joyful feeling through this process.

(My thanks to Nora Birch who taught me this visualization in her meditation class.)

Visualization: Looking Into The Lake.

Find a safe comfortable place to sit or lie down. Play some soft meditative music. You could see yourself in a meadow or a field. Whatever works for you. Take a few breaths, breathing in and out slowly and easily. Feel the body relax more and more with each inhalation and exhalation. Feel more and more at ease and peaceful. Now imagine you are standing at a lake. Take in your surroundings. Maybe you hear some nature sounds, or the laughter of children's voices. Notice how calm and quiet the lake is. It is smooth and clear as a mirror. As you look into the lake notice some reflections. You may see images of trees and the clouds rolling by You also notice your reflection in this lake. Notice your aura as you see yourself reflected back to you. What colours do you see around your image? If you cannot see the colours, get a sense of what these colours would be. Some identify the colours by how they feel. By this I mean, does the colour feel warm or cool? Warm colours are generally associated with the colours of red, orange and yellow. And the cooler sensations are the blues, indigo and violets. So how does it feel around you, does it feel cool or warm? This may help you to get a sense of what colours are emanating from your chakras.

Now imagine yourself stepping into the lake and into your reflection Feel yourself merging with your reflection. And blend your physical body with your aura now. Notice how that feels. Take some time to experience the merging of the physical body and the reflection. Now see if you can expand your aura. Get a sense of expanding it to the ends of the lake. Now imagine that you are drawing your field close to you. Draw it back in towards your physical body. Now just relax and let the aura find its own comfortable place. Take a few moments to allow that settling in to happen.

Now take your hands and scoop up some water and pour this water over you. Repeat this action over and over again. As you scoop the water and pour it all over yourself, imagine you are cleaning your field.

Now step back out of the water and allow the water to become quiet and smooth again. Then notice if the colours of your aura have changed. Are they more brilliant? What do you see or sense now? Has your field expanded? How do you feel now? When you are ready, take your time and come back into the space.

Exercises

1) You may want to draw the colours in the aura you saw, both before and after.

2) Write how you were feeling at the beginning of the exercise and how you feel now.

3) Decide to use the image of the calm lake to quiet your mind to make yourself feel good.

4) Decide to use this visualization to centre yourself and bring balance to your busy life.

Student Comments

"These teachings have given me insight into the messages my body was giving me. I am now aware that when I felt stressed and had negative thoughts; my body reacted by manifesting bladder problems, bloating and feeling weighted down. This was all due to the fact that I was not happy, and I did not feel loved and worthy. Since changing my beliefs about myself, I am noticing such a difference in my health. I feel much lighter, more balanced, I love myself and others more and I have so much more energy to do the things I like to do. I bounce and dance through my day. And I notice I am attracting more happy people into my life since I am more joyful. Thanks Marlene, for your encouragement along my joyous path. My health gets better and better everyday." N.W.

Synopsis

Be Happy, Feel Happy, Make Others Happy, Too!

Our Bodies Are A Mirror Of Our Mind.

Now that you know that, be more careful where your emotions lead you When you feel yourself sliding into old habits of sadness, anger and resentment, simply say "STOP!" Use that word as a trigger to refocus your attention to a vision, a memory, a piece of music that makes you happy. When discomfort occurs, refer to the chakras to help you determine the source of the discomfort. If it progresses to pain, be sure to consult your medical practitioner to allow them to help you heal. That does not relieve you of your responsibility to partner with him or her by tending to your emotional and spiritual health while he treats your physical body. The chakras are a map of your body provided by the universe to help you heal and stay healthy. Right now, in this moment, appreciate the goodness behind the guidance to your continued good health.

ACKNOWLEDGING PETER INMAN: A powerful healer who used advanced forms of transformational energy healing techniques, some chiropractic practices, psychic surgery, energy clearing, lectures and invocations. He learned his work from many Mexican healers.

50,000
20,000
100,000,00

chapter Eight

Money, Business, Success

Joyous Living Skill #8: It is your birthright to have success. Believe it is possible. The universe will bring it to you. Let's get started!

In Western culture, many of us define success in terms of our personal wealth. However, the amount of our assets is less important than how we feel about them. One man's concept of poverty is another man's gracious plenty. It is impossible to put a numerical value on success which will suit everyone. With that in mind, let's shift our focus from a specific goal to the process of achieving it. Given the universe is perfect, we get back what we put in. Therefore, it is important we only put in good things in order to get good things out. Referring to the previous chapters, our relationship with our assets is like our relationship with our self and others. Clean up the relationship with yourself and the other relationships will fall into place, eventually creating abundance where there once was scarcity.

Your shift in consciousness will occur when you are ready. Once you are committed to do so the process is very simple. Create a list of what you do not want. It helps to generate the positive feelings you want to associate with this "want list." Lastly, allow it to happen. It often helps to cross out the items on the "do not want" list to help you generate the positive feelings you want to associate with the "want list." As before, it's not the mind that takes care of this particular bit of business, it's your emotions. Smile when you write down your "want list," smile wider when you send it out to the universe with the expectation it will be fulfilled.

Create a list of possibilities which to you feels possible. What is possible depends on your willingness to do what it takes to get it. You will not win the lottery if you do not buy a ticket. Be specific on what you want. For example, don't ask for a steady income of $1,000,000 a month, if you know that amount of money will make you uncomfortable. Does it make me uncomfortable because it is too much money or because I do not believe I will achieve it? Do ask for a monthly income which is within your comfort zone. Baby steps for now will lead to giant steps later. Trust that the universe has gotten you where you are so far, so that you are now in the perfect place to create some positive changes in your life, and attract more of what you want for two big reasons. You believe it will happen, and it feels good.

My Story

As I look back over my life I realize that each job and hobby was in some way preparing me for the role I carry out in my career today. My dancing days (ages 4-16) were filled with creative expression coaching my classmates. The hair styling business I owned and operated in South Africa from the age of 17 to 25 taught me how to become an effective business owner. My jobs after immigrating to Canada required interpersonal skills. I worked at a health facility, then at a bank as a teller in foreign exchange, and in stocks and bonds. After that I worked at a university and in real estate before entering the wellness area. During these years I took business and psychology courses. I also studied fine arts at a university. It was during my years in real estate that I began to study the alterative health field. Simultaneously, I began to work on my own self-healing. This important decision led me to many supportive people who assisted me on my quest to heal.

At times, change can be painful. But the benefits far outweigh the discomfort of transforming. In the end, we feel more alive, happier and healthier. One of my teachers once asked me, "Marlene, when will you be enough? How many more courses do you need to take to begin your work?" That day I made another important decision in my life. I was ready to share with people what I had learned.

I started my first Healing Circle teaching four people to learn to love and value themselves. It is said we teach what we need to learn. At that time in my life, I was still learning to love and appreciate me. Soon the number of people attending grew. Many changes took place over the years. I noticed that as I transformed and changed, so did my work. Then I taught lessons on transforming relationships. At that time I was being challenged with regard to my relationships.

When challenges arose in my business I learned to take responsibility for what I manifested. I did not blame the economy, the government, or the clients. I always looked to myself first. I examined where I had focused my thoughts and what was my attitude to what was happening. I know that my willingness to own and be responsible for what is happening has greatly contributed to my business success.

I reached a point when I did not want to work so many weekends. I had been doing this for over 15 years. I decided I wanted to have fun on some weekends. I wanted to spend more time doing things with my husband and family. Many times I had had to turn down invitations because I had to work. I mostly wanted to have more weekends free in the summer to play golf, have picnics, spend time outdoors and go away for fun-filled weekends. I also put out strong, clear intentions to the universe about the kinds of people that I now wanted to work with. In the meantime, my partner and I were getting clearer and clearer about our intentions for our future. This included a possible move, buying homes in two different countries, and working towards handing my husband's business over to our son. We were asking for and planning so much.

Over a period of time, I noticed a definite decrease in the number of my clients and workshop participants. I started to question this, but then I realized that I asked the universe to send to me a particular group of people. The ones who were coming to me were exactly the ones I was asking to work with. They were people with a strong commitment to fulfill their desires, and work consistently with the skills. The universe heard my request, and sent me those who fulfilled this intention. I was getting exactly what I wanted. I also asked for ways to reach larger audiences or to spend a segment of my time with more than one person outside of my regular workshops, seminars and teleconferences. The other request I made was to work less and create more money. This is unfolding nicely through this book and my tapes and CDs. So I had to remind myself that this is exactly what I wanted, and that I was right on schedule. Everything was unfolding perfectly.

How Our Personal Lives Affect Our Business/money/success

Many of us do not realize that what is happening in our business lives in many ways relates to what goes on in our personal lives. We tend to feel that one is exclusive of the other. This has become more and more evident to me over the years. During my sessions with my clients they realize that the challenges they have in their personal lives are carried into the work environment.

If we have unresolved issues with mom, dad, siblings and past significant relationships, we will be placed in situations where we find ourselves having challenges with others who will represent these people. This is the universe offering us the opportunity to heal and transform these unhealthy relationships to create space for healthy ones.

Dorothy's Story

Dorothy's father was very strict. He set high standards for her. One minute he was praising her and the next moment he would judge her. This confused Dorothy because, one minute she was feeling good about herself, and then she was feeling bad. When her father saw her happy, he would find some reason to yell at her. This frustrated and angered her. His behaviour also made her feel insecure and stupid.

She lived her life always in anticipation that something bad was going to happen, particularly when she was having a good day. Her belief continued to confirm her thinking. Invariably something bad always followed something good.

When Dorothy went out to work, she seemed to attract bosses who treated her the same way her father did. One minute they were telling her what a great job she did, and then they would call her into the office to criticize her work. This reception by her bosses resulted in Dorothy going from one job to another. But nothing changed because of Dorothy's insecure feelings and her belief that all her bosses treated her the same. Dorothy finally sought help, and in a very short time she realized that she needed to change how she felt about her father's behavior, and therefore her beliefs about how her bosses treated her. Then she was able to move forward.

It is not about how hard you work. It is about how you are feeling about your work that counts. If working hard feels good, then continue. However, if it becomes a frustration and it feels like a struggle, you may want to step back and revisit your vision of what it is you truly want for yourself. Imagine yourself doing your job joyously. Then set yourself some new steps, steps which inspire you to take the action to accomplish what you say you want. Sometimes we have our vision all written out. Then we go into action and lose ourselves in the process. Inspired action is the key.

It is more about taking inspired action rather than forcing yourself to do something that does not feel good. First set out your intentions. Then let the universe give you a nudge to proceed with the action. You will know when to proceed because you will feel excited about moving into the action.

I have had a few clients who go on many job interviews and can't seem to get the one they want. After discussing with them what kind of job they want, it is clear that they have not set their vision as to what they would like to experience in their future job. If they don't know what they want, how can they expect to be hired by someone who knows what they are looking for in an employee?

Our first step is to get clear on what we want, and why we want it. Then ask and trust that your source is bringing it to you.

Betty's Story

Betty hated her job. Getting up for work in the morning was a chore. When at work she was agitated and short with the people she interacted with. She complained about the people, her boss, and the office. Nothing at work pleased her. Betty talked about the challenges she was having in her personal relationships, especially her mate. With further questioning it became clear that another reason why she was feeling dissatisfied was due to some changes in her duties at work. Betty was not feeling confident about the new projects that she was recently assigned. This task required that she now interact and work within a team.

When Betty was first hired to work at the company, she worked independently. This is what she liked most, and was one of the main reasons she decided to work at this firm. She is a self-starter and prefers to work on her own. Betty's social skills are not her strongest asset. Since these changes in her job requirements have occurred, Betty has been feeling insecure about her work.

Betty now realizes that nothing can change for her until she changes how she is feeling about herself when she is at work, and also about how she feels about her relationship with her partner.

1) Betty wrote pages and pages of things she liked and appreciated about herself.

2) She also wrote a list of the things she appreciated about her work, the other employees and the new tasks she was assigned.

3) She wrote a list of appreciative things she liked about her mate.

4) When she was at home she would appreciate her job, her boss and the people she worked with.

5) She would visualize herself working as a team with her co-workers with everyone loving what they were doing to contribute to the project.

How Low Self-esteem And Feeling Unworthy Affects Our Success

If you have a belief that you are not good enough, or if you have low self-esteem, you will not be as successful as you would like to be. As in Betty's case above, she felt she worked better independently, but circumstances forced her in a team situation. It was not that she couldn't do the work as well; she felt that she couldn't work well in a group. So she didn't. Her self-esteem affected her performance. Another client's esteem issues translated itself into monetary losses. In his own words:

"In the early eighties I had a 20% partner and the business was doing extremely well. The beginning of 1989 I bought out my partner. Then in the spring of 1989 I lost our largest account, which represented about 75% of my business. I realized now, that when the first large account was lost I never got over that fully, even though the business improved. I always had the insecure feeling that maybe this situation would repeat itself again. And as the universe never fails to deliver to us the evidence of what we think, feel and focus on, it is clear to me now why we lost the second account.

In order to move forward I visualized my new career (doing what I did before, but on my own with no employees). I also talked to the universe expressing what it is I now wanted for my relationships, family and my prosperity. I decided to not think about what happened in the past, I placed my attention on how I was feeling about my life now, making sure I was feeling good as I thought about what I wanted for myself for my future. The business was doing fine, but I was not feeling fulfilled anymore. I now had lost all my enthusiasm and I started to think about moving on to something new.

As soon as I took my attention off the daily grind of the present business I started to focus and imagine myself in this new job. I started to feel more secure, with the result my present business has boomed to the point where I now feel I need to find people to assist me with the sudden influx of business. By starting to feel passionate about what is to come in the future with the new career, success seems to be in my grasp. But at the same time I feel like I am putting myself on hold because although I now want to move toward this new project, I have created this increase and success in my present company. This financial success is what I have been wanting for so long, but present family financial responsibilities require (so I feel) that I now nurture and attend to the work at hand." E.D.

Another client believed that hard work was always a requirement for success. In fact, without working hard there would be no success. Certainly, working hard contributes to success for those who hold that belief, but we all know of people who achieve success effortlessly, as well as those who work hard and never make it. The difference is how they feel about their success, which is ultimately how they feel about themselves.

Client's Comments

"I somehow felt that I had to work hard for what I got. I had to feel the pain to actually be successful and that is exactly what I did. Through learning I now know that this was not the case. The last four years of my life have changed drastically. I now understand that you get what you think about, whether you want it or not. I now no longer give my attention to matters that I do not want to occur, but I instead hold the vision of those things that I do want to occur. My life today is very different in that things come very easy for me and success is greater than I imagined. I now understand that there is abundance out there and it does not matter what others do as it will have no effect on me as long as I do my own envisioning on what I am wanting." M.T.

How Feelings of Lack About Money Will Affect Our Success

If we hold beliefs that we have to work hard to earn money, we will always have to work hard to have a comfortable life. If we feel lack about money, we will never have enough money.

For some of us money is a big worry and concern. These people may have all the money they wish, but do not truly enjoy their wealth. They may buy many material things, but underlying all of this, they are unhappy. They do not give to themselves or to others.

Others always seem to have enough, and are contented with what they have. For some having $1,000.00 in the bank feels comfortable. Others may need $10,000.00 to feel comfortable and happy.

The same can apply to work and success. Some people are happy doing what may seem to someone else a menial job. If this person is content then he will continue in the same place until he retires. For others there is a strong need to expand and move up the corporate ladder. Neither is right or wrong. The most important thing is that they are happy while they wait for their desires to be fulfilled. For when they are happy, they will each be able to attract more of what they want, and through this continue to lead happy lives.

At times people have owed me money. The more I focused on the fact that they owed me money, and the more I worried about it and talked to others about it, the more I noticed it did not make me feel good to have to beg these people to pay me back. I would leave them messages asking for my money. Many of them ignored my calls, or promised me that they were placing it in the mail. Needless to say the cheque did not arrive.

During the time I was giving this subject so much attention, I noticed that my business was slowing down. Fewer people attended my classes, fewer clients called for appointments and unexpected bills also arrived in the mail. Finally, I realized what I was doing: I was focused on lack. This meant I was a match to lack. And if I continued to stay focused on the lack of money, the money these people owed me would not come.

As soon as I realized what I was doing, referrals came to me. Many of my clients that I had not seen for a while called to see me. Cheques came in the mail from people who owed me money that I had forgotten about. Some clients paid me more than my regular fee, and my workshops increased.

The money could not come when my thinking and feelings were, "I cannot get my money from these people."

1) All I had to do was talk more about the money being on its way to me, such as "Soon I will have my money." Or "These people have full intentions of paying me." I did not focus on the people who were not paying me. All I needed to do was talk more in the positive about the money coming to me.

2) I could also have visualized the money coming in the mail.

3) Visualized myself depositing the money.

4) Know that my request has been heard.

5) Trust that they will eventually pay.

Olivia's Story

As a child Olivia had many bad dreams. Since her home was somewhat dysfunctional and she felt detached from her mother, Olivia always felt anxious and fearful. As an adult she experienced bankruptcy. All along Olivia was working on herself. She used many of these skills, went to workshops, healing and counseling. When she was faced with major challenges around her job, her relationships, and especially money, she was always able to dig deep down inside herself. There she found her own inner strength, wisdom and guidance. This helped her to get beyond the anger and fear that she was holding. It also got her ego and pride out of the way, so that the universe could deliver to her what she was now wanting in her life.

She realizes now that although she was asking, what she wanted could not come because of the underlining fears and anxieties she still felt at times.

What she started to realize was that when she felt lack around money she started to ask and talk more specifically about what she wanted, i.e. to receive some quick closings in her real estate business, to receive some property listings, to receive referrals, and most of all, to sell the properties she listed. It started to dawn on her that she is being taken care of, that when she asked and expected it to come, it came; many times without physical effort on her part. This helped her to relax and to feel less fearful. She now trusts and knows that what she wants will always come to her as long as she relaxes, stays happy and has no doubt that what she asks for is on its way to her.

Because she has all the skills she needs, when she now has any major challenge, it is easier for her to start trusting and turning her attention to what she wants. She spends money on herself. If she sees something that she wants, she now feels deserving of it.

How Fear of Success/failure Affects Our Success

If we fear success and/or fear failure, fear will become our reality.

I am sure that my insecurities regarding the writing of this book have to do with my fear of failure. Will people like the book? Will it be successful?

Steven's Story

Steven was a vice principal of a school. Whenever the opportunity arose for him to move to the position of principal, he would create a circumstance that prevented him from receiving the position. In everyone else's eyes, he was highly intelligent and capable. They assumed that he could easily get the position. Steven, on the other hand, felt a little insecure. He did not feel capable of actually being a success in the position. His co-workers were not aware of the fear that he harboured.

As a young child he was told that he was stupid, dumb and would never amount to anything. This voice of his father always rings in his ears, especially when something important to him materializes.

Steven has been receiving guidance on how to move past these old beliefs and perceptions.

Mandy's Story

Mandy works in real estate. Many times she did not have a lot of desire to work. She would sell a few houses, and then relax in the knowing that she has some income to tide her over a period. She also suffered from depression, due to a feeling of loneliness and physical pain. This added to her lack of work ethic.

On the other hand, when the depression passed, she had tremendous energy and desire to go back to work. Twice she sold five homes in rapid succession, totaling ten homes in a very short period of time. When this happened, she knew she could make the sales, and felt very confident and in charge. She realizes that she has a fear of success, so in many ways she sabotages herself. Now she also realizes that when she was in the place of lack, and feeling lonely, she created that her parents would rally around, and rescue her. They would encourage her to get back to her work, and then she would get back on track again.

Now that she is more conscious of the dynamics of her relationship to her work, she no longer relies on her parents to inspire her. She now finds it within herself to get motivated and passionate about her life and work. When she acts, it is because she loves to do her work, which is finding the perfect home for her clients. Because she is feeling better about herself, her relationship with her parents has improved.

One of her main goals was to own her own cottage up north on the lake which will be her retirement place. She has since manifested her dream cottage on the lake.

If we are successful by our own definition of success, we have ourselves to thank for it. We were fortunate enough to know exactly what we wanted, felt good about it, and then put it out to the universe with every expectation of getting it. If we are still seeking success, again we have only ourselves to blame for it. We need to shift our focus from sorrow and shame, to hope for our future, for that is the only way we will have what we want, and be able to enjoy it when we get it.

My Story

Earlier in my healing, before I understood how I attracted things into my experience, I worked at a company for seven years. I loved my job, but I found myself in a situation where I got fired. At the time I could not understand why this was happening to me. The head of the department never complained about my work, so needless to say when the complaints started coming in, I was stunned. My immediate supervisor made my life miserable. She continued to judge my work. I started to get paranoid, thinking that they set traps for me to fail. I started to feel more and more insecure, and then made more and more mistakes with my work. I felt like a victim. I even created spraining my ankle as a way to stay home, and not have to face the pressure I felt she was placing on me. This was not a conscious decision, but my desire was very strong at the time to not to have to go to work and face the stress. I finally was asked to leave, or transfer to another area in the company, and that was a very sad day for me. I loved my work, and I could not understand why this was happening to me.

I had many sleepless nights and bad dreams. My self- confidence was low. Then I earned my license to sell real estate and did that for five years. In the meantime, I continued on my journey to self-healing. Through these programs, I started to realize that a lot of what happened to me was because of my own thoughts and feelings. The more she found fault with me, the more insecure I felt. I was the perfect victim. The more I told everyone who would listen to my sad story, the more likely it was that nothing was going to change for me. I realized that it was not her. Yes, she was doing what she was doing, but most importantly, it was myself, my thoughts, feelings, and how much I was focusing on this problem that brought the whole situation to its climax. The only thing that could happen here was that I was bringing this job loss upon myself. I know that I created the outcome I received. Ultimately I was responsible for it.

We must be willing to take ownership for our part in what we are creating. We must be conscious of where we focus with regard to what we want and change how we feel about the situation, the people and ourselves. We must focus on feeling better. Your power is in the now. If you continue to feel that way, nothing is going to change. In order to bring about change, you have to change your thoughts and feelings to something that feels a little better. Eventually, you will move yourself to a place where you are feeling more in charge and happier. The universe will then be able to bring you what you want. Your source wants you to have whatever you desire, be happy and live a joy-filled life. We deserve to have it all.

If we think about our business, job, money or success, and we are not feeling good about these topics, we will only continue to create more frustrations and challenges for ourselves.

In order for us to attract more of what we want, we need to take our attention off the problem. Discuss only the things about your business that make you feel good in the company. If you have nothing good to say about your business, it is best to focus on something else which feels better. Stop your worrying about the bills you cannot pay. Remember a time when things were going well.

Which feels better? Worrying about a sale that did not occur, or going to pet your dog or cat?

Which feels better? Worrying about an employee who is not performing well or to remember a time when he/she did something well?

Which feels better? Worrying about the business or your job, or leaving the office to play a game of golf? If you are having trouble taking your attention off the concerns around the business, you would serve yourself and your company better not to go in that day and find other more pleasant and fun things to do. You may find by doing so, meaning taking your focus and thoughts off the challenges in the company and living yourself up, that good things will start to happen again. This occurs because you have let go of your resistance.

The universe knows your desires with regard to the business or your job. When things are not going well, ask the universe to change things for the better. Then all you have to do is find ways to feel good.

1) WE TEND TO TAKE ONE THING IN OUR LIVES AND GIVE IT OUR FULL ATTENTION. HOWEVER, THERE ARE SO MANY OTHER THINGS OUT THERE WE CAN FOCUS ON TO FEEL GOOD.

2) WE ALSO PLACE SO MUCH UNDUE PRESSURE ON OURSELVES BY COMPARING OURSELVES WITH OTHERS.

3) THE POWER POINT IS THE PRESENT: turn the page on the past, forget the future. Right now, today, focus on what you want and feel the joy in getting it.

Visualization

Find a place where you can get comfortable. Breathe in to the count of 4 some long deep breaths. Hold for the count of 5 and then exhale for the count of 4. Repeat this 3 more times. While exhaling, feel the body softening more and more. Now think of some things in your life that you can appreciate. It may be your children, your beautiful garden, the wonderful meal you just ate, or the clerk at the grocery store. Just allow your mind to wander from one appreciative thought to another. Think of all the wonderful things about your life now: your family, your job or past great jobs and your health. Even if you can only think of one thing to appreciate on a particular subject, that is where I want your mind to be. Notice how different and lighter your body feels. Your concerns and problems now seem to be a distant memory.

Once you are joyous, more relaxed and feeling more invigorated, imagine that five years have gone by. You are living and enjoying whatever goals you had set for yourself. See yourself successful. You may not have acquired everything yet. But you are comfortable and looking forward to what is on its way to you. You are feeling so appreciative of what you have attracted so far. And you are happy in your now just enjoying what you are doing. You feel comfortable and proud of what you have accomplished so far. You love coming to this place to build and expand on your dreams but most importantly you take this time for yourself because it feels good. You cannot wait to come back another time to play and enjoy your vision. You are contented in the knowing that what you have asked for is on its way to you. In the meantime, you move through your day with ease, trusting that the universe will continue to bring you what you have been asking for.

You feel comfortable and appreciative about your finances. You are also appreciative of the job that you have, or the past jobs you attained. Continue to bliss out in the fantasy of your life now and the possibility of all the good that is on its way to you. When you are ready, come back and bring with you all those wonderful feelings of appreciation and wonder of what is on its way to you.

Exercises

1) Write down all the things you appreciate. Add to your list any new things that come to mind during this visualization.

2) Sketch any images that come to you.

3) Add to your list of goals anything new that comes to you about money, business or success.

4) Make a list of all your business clients you appreciate. You could also send them a note if you wish.

5) Journal and add new ideas that came to you.

6) Add more to your want list.

7) Mail yourself a "congratulations on your success" note.

8) Mail yourself an invitation to an awards presentation where you will be the guest of honor.

I may have inspired you with some ideas and you now may want to add some more of your own.

THE ABOVE SUGGESTIONS APPLY TO MONEY, SUCCESS AND BUSINESS, BUT THE SKILLS ARE THE SAME IN ALL AREAS OF OUR LIVES. WHAT WE THINK AND WORRY ABOUT WE WILL CREATE AND ATTRACT INTO OUR BUSINESS.

FIND WAYS TO RECENTRE YOURSELF, REMEMBER WHAT IT IS WE WANT AND TRUST THAT IT IS ON ITS WAY TO YOU. YOUR JOB IS TO GET HAPPY AND STAY HAPPY.

Just For Fun: Visualization For Creating Money.

IMAGINE YOURSELF COUNTING AS MANY DOLLAR BILLS AS YOU WISH (SOME COUNT $20 BILLS, SOME $100 BILLS, AND SOME COUNT $1000 BILLS.) THEN SEE YOURSELF PILING THE BILLS IN INDIVIDUAL PILES AND FILLING IN THE DEPOSIT SLIP. SEE YOURSELF ENTERING THE BANK, GOING UP TO THE TELLER. WATCH AS SHE PUTS THE DOLLARS THROUGH THE COUNTING MACHINE.SHE THEN UPDATES YOUR BANK BOOK, AND HANDS YOU YOUR BOOK. YOU LOOK AT THE NEW BALANCE AND YOU ARE NOW FEELING SO THRILLED AND PROSPEROUS AS YOU WALK BACK TO YOUR CAR. AS YOU DRIVE AWAY YOU START TO THINK ABOUT SPENDING THIS IMAGINARY MONEY ON THINGS THAT YOU WANT.

YOU CAN REPEAT THE SAME PROCESS OVER AND OVER AGAIN TAKING IN DIFFERENT AMOUNTS TO DEPOSIT INTO YOUR ACCOUNT. YOU COULD LEAVE IT THERE FOR A WHILE OR START TO IMAGINE SPENDING IT ON THE ANYTHING THAT YOU DESIRE.

THE MOST IMPORTANT THING HERE IS TO PLAY THIS GAME FOR THE PLEASURE IT BRINGS YOU.

"Your Invisible Power: A Presentation of the Mental Science of Thomas Troward" by Genevieve Behrend.

Student comments

"My sessions with Marlene have brought me so much peace of mind, good health, fabulous relationships and successful partnerships in another business. I have also come to the point where I feel more deserving and worthy to have all the things that I want. These sessions led me to an awakening. Although I always had no doubt that one day I would be successful and live a full happy life. I was not aware of my underlying beliefs that I did not deserve such riches.

Prior to this new business, I sold my partnership in my marketing company. This business, at times, was very challenging and, at that time, I believed that hard work led to success. As I worked hard, I ignored the part of my soul that loved to travel. Once I finally gave myself permission to do so, I was able to make myself feel good and to manage the challenges in the company. This business finally came to a conclusion as I applied the tools of visualization. I visualized myself attaining closure in my business relationships and with the company. In the meantime, I began creating the new venture. The most important part was that I continued to have no doubts that what I wanted would come.

I now live a life of opulence. I have vacationed in many exotic places, stayed in grand hotels, eaten at the best of restaurants. I wear the finest clothes and jewellery, live in a beautiful home, have a wonderful relationship and support many worthy causes. My life is wonderful and I look forward to many more delightful things." E.G.

Synopsis

If we want to attract more money into our lives, the first thing we need to understand is how we draw to ourselves situations, and events and the money we want into our lives. We do this through placing our attention. What we focus on and the emotion we feel, can and will draw more of the same to you. "Like attracts like." So if you are focused on lack of money, you cannot have abundance in your life. More money cannot come. Switch your thoughts and feelings to a thing that will make you feel better about money.

In order to manifest more money into your life you have to speak about money in a more positive way. Instead of saying "I cannot afford this now" say "One day soon I will be able to purchase this." This changes how you now feel about the subject of money. Consciously choose your thoughts, words and feelings so that they can go in the direction of what you are now wanting. In regard to speaking and thinking more about what you do not want, focus more on what you want and why you want it.

And then relax, be joyful and trust that what you are asking for is on its way to you. The easiest way to do this is through appreciation.

Use these same theories if you want to have a healthy body, healthier relationships and anything else you desire.

chapter Nine

Forever Young
Why we want eternal youth.

JOYOUS LIVING SKILL #9: SMILE MORE! LAUGH MORE! DANCE MORE! AND YOUR BODY WILL MIRROR THAT BACK TO YOU!

Many explorers have unsuccessfully devoted their lives to finding the fountain of youth. We live in times where so much emphasis is placed on looking good and having a beautiful body, it is little wonder youth or the appearance of youth is a primary cultural value. We focus on our diets and eating healthy food. We hold models and movie stars in high esteem for their beauty. The plastic surgery industry thrives. Today, many of our youth set unrealistic standards for themselves regarding their looks based on this cultural value. Some of them pay a high emotional and physical price to manifest and maintain these unrealistic appearances. Young and old, we direct our attention to our external appearance rather than our internal health. I have personally been down that road and anorexia almost took my life.

Considering we pursue this youthful ideal, why do so many people look older than they are?

This obsession is a result of their thoughts, feelings and beliefs about aging. Today, more people fear growing old more than they fear death Because we observed people before us decline, we believe that this has to be our future. The media bombards us with information on health and growing old. The sad part is that their facts are scare tactics without regard to the effects the information has on the audience. If eternal youth is our cultural ideal, then aging must be our cultural evil. With so much emphasis placed on youth, we feel a moral obligation to stay young, or give the appearance of youth, regardless of our chronological age. Since the clock continues to tick, regardless of our actions, hopes or wishes, we live under continuous stress because of our failure to control that which cannot be controlled.

As I discussed in the chapter on Health, the body follows the mind. If you are feeling young, regardless of the date of your birth, your body will follow, producing a young healthy body. But if you believe you will grow old fast, your body will give you the evidence to confirm your feeling. Culturally, we suffer a double whammy: don't get old, and if you do, look and act young. The result is: Fear + Stress = Premature Aging

Your internal image will become your appearance, your body in height and size. The exact image that you hold in your mind, and how you feel about that image, will appear as your physical evidence. Even when we were younger, many of us hated what we saw when we looked in the mirror. As we age, our self-loathing increases. All the exercise and surgery, diets and supplements cannot fool Mother Nature, or your real self. Allow your real self to change your attitude and see how much more attractive that face in the mirror is when it looks back at you.

My Anorexia Story

In my early teens, I always felt fat. To add to my insecurity about my weight, my friends and my family constantly commented on my fat face and plump body. This really angered me. So one day I decided that I was going to lose weight and show them all. I started to diet, and for days I barely ate a thing. People started to tell me how good I looked. These compliments enhanced my feelings of low self-esteem, and the many doubts I had about myself.

Even though I started to lose many pounds, when I looked in the mirror, the image looking back at me always appeared fat. Consequently, no matter how much weight I lost, it was never enough. I felt fat and imperfect. All the comments about how good I looked were not enough to fill the void I felt inside. I went down to 83 pounds on a 5 foot tall frame. When I look back at that time, I realize that getting married and leaving home seemed to be the cure which allowed me to return to a healthier lifestyle. Two years later the birth of our son, and the focus on my business made me feel loved and needed, and gave me reasons to live.

Soon after that, I started on my quest for self-healing. I took many courses, read many books, and listened to many tapes. I enrolled in business, human relations, psychology, and alternative courses over the years These teachings and programs helped me to feel better about myself. My studies provided me with skills to maintain my body at optimum health. I learned to forgive myself and others and to accept everything that comes my way as a perfect expression of my unfolding life.

The internal image and the message I now give my body is a healthy, energetic, strong, lean and shapely muscle mass; shiny hair; smooth, firm and glowing skin, perfect eyesight and acute hearing; strong, healthy teeth, gums, and strong bones. Daily I send my body the same message: for every cell in my body to rejuvenate and come back into complete balance and harmony when I rest.

How we think and feel about our bodies will be what our bodies manifest and show us. So if we want our bodies to produce the evidence of what we want, we have to hold the image of the kind of physical body we want to produce. As expressed here, the body follows what the mind feels is possible. You must ask for what you want with regard to your physical health, and then believe that you can attain it. Then relax and let the body do its part.

Elizabeth's Story:

Elizabeth always had a slim frame. As she grew older she maintained this size. She had an internal clock and an image she held of herself into her adult life.

As she entered her menopausal years, she continued to maintain her slim body, but her overall health was in a slow decline. Elizabeth had many personal and work stresses. This stress caused her body to slowly deteriorate. She paid more attention to how she was physically feeling about her body. She also talked to anyone who would listen to her about her failing health and her personal problems.

The more she talked about her failing health, the more her body provided her with the evidence to confirm her thinking. She received a prescription for her stress and for menopause. Although this remedy did help to soothe the symptoms, not much changed, because Elizabeth bought into the belief that her body was slowly deteriorating as it aged.

It is about how we feel about ourselves and our bodies that counts. We cannot feel forever young, if we believe in growing old.

Exercise

This exercise will help you discover how you are feeling about your body and yourself.

First, write down all the things you like about yourself: For instance, "My hair, my eyes, my nose, my creativity, my intelligence and my laughter."

Now, take a moment to write down what it would be like to feel forever young. See yourself full of energy and happiness, leading an interesting, passionate life.

1)

2)

3)

4)

1) ARE YOU READY TO TAKE THIS LEAP OF FAITH TODAY?
2) ARE YOU OPEN TO THE POSSIBILITY OF HAVING WHAT YOU WANT BECOME A REALITY?
3) ARE READY TO BELIEVE IT BEFORE YOU SEE IT?

If your answer is yes, there is no room for doubt.

1) First we have to ask for what we want.
2) Feel good about yourself while you wait for your request to manifest.
3) Trust that what you have asked for is on its way to you.

We will continue this exercise later.

For many, no amount of dieting, exercise or plastic surgery will give them a permanent change. There have been studies on people who have had plastic surgery to beautify themselves. Those with low self-esteem continue to return for more work, because no amount of work is ever enough. Even though their outward appearance changed, they were still not satisfied with their new look, because they did not feel good about themselves inwardly. Making outward changes is not enough; they have to start with changing their beliefs and feelings about themselves first.

For some, making the outward changes first makes it easier for them to start loving themselves. The new image in the mirror gives them the opportunity to feel better about themselves and their bodies, and with that new confidence the body maintains the picture that is reflected back to them in the mirror. The difference is in how they are feeling about themselves.

They love the changes in their appearance. These changes are enough to help them feel better about themselves, and create desire to maintain this new look. By changing how they feel about their bodies, and believing that they can look beautiful, this now changes their internal feelings. This is the catalyst that assists the body in producing a beautiful outward image of itself.

For example, many women who are beautiful do not feel attractive. In their minds they feel ugly. No matter how many people tell them that they are beautiful, they have trouble accepting the compliment. Again, this stems from their childhood. They respond in this way because they were told they were ugly, worthless and stupid. It is little wonder that they have difficulty feeling beautiful. As soon as they change their negative feelings to positive ones, their bodies will respond in accordance with their feelings and then they will feel attractive.

As soon as you determine your story, be prepared to leave it in the past where it began. When we were little, we trusted and thought our parents and peers knew what was best for us. We forgot we have our own guidance system. That system is very simple: Good feels good, and bad feels bad Does it feel good to hate your body? Think negatively of yourself? Reject the physical manifestation of our spirit, our soul?

Understand that the statistics for body standards are just someone else's perception of perfection. What is right for them does not have to be how we choose to live our lives. Let's not be so quick to judge ourselves.

Some of the things you want for yourself, you may want to keep to yourself. If you let others know what your dreams are, and they don't think it's possible, they may try to talk you out of them. If you are not confident that you can have the things you want, you may let their story destroy yours.

Many of my clients say they want to be healthy and have more energy, but all they do is talk negatively about themselves and their bodies. They can't get what they want by doing this. The universe does not care how much money you spend on spas, diets, lotions, oils or medications If you do not like yourself or your body, you will only attract a temporary, superficial change.

I am not saying that there is anything wrong with exercising and doing things to improve your health and looks to beautify yourself. Rather I am saying it's about where you place most of your thoughts and your feelings on the subject.

For another example, let's consider illness. If you and your sibling grew up in the same family where someone was ill, one of you may grow up assuming illness is a way of life. Both of you observed the illness, listened to the daily conversations focused on the illness, and experienced the other person's illness because you were exposed to it within your family. It is possible for one of you to become ill because of your belief that illness is inevitable, whereas the other may live a full and healthy life. The healthy member of the family realized that the illness belonged to the person who was suffering, and did not pertain to them.

Their beliefs regarding their feelings about illness determined the outcome. The same theory applies to weight challenges. Why do some members of the same family have weight challenges and others do not? It's not so much about the food we eat, as about how we feel when we eat the food. If you eat cake and believe you will gain weight, this will be your experience. However, if you eat the cake and enjoy it, without thinking whether this action makes a difference in your weight, you will receive a double bonus: eating your cake and enjoying it, too - without a weight penalty.

When we buy into the belief that certain foods are bad for us, we allow that belief to be true. I overhear people at a dessert counter saying, "I better not eat this. It will make me fat." With this thinking, they will gain weight, because their thoughts will produce those results.

In the first chapter we discussed "the leap of faith" I asked you to make in order to actualize the promises expressed in this book. Again, please put aside your intellectual side, your internal censor and allow the universe to show you that this is possible.

If there is a specific illness in your family, and you believe you will succumb to it, you will draw it into your life. Your thoughts and feelings will become your experience. Many of my clients have a history of heart attacks in their family. Now they live in constant fear of having a heart attack. If they continue to think this way, they will more than likely have the experience. By the same token, if someone in the family decides that this will not happen to them, that they intend to remain healthy, they will not experience a heart attack. Is it not in the genes? Knowing what we now know: we attract to ourselves what we believe about a subject

My Story: Forever Young

I attribute my perfect health to my parents. I thank them for this. As a child growing up in our household, I had to be truly ill to be allowed to stay home. This also applied to my two sisters. Both my parents were very dedicated to their work. I do not remember my father ever taking time off from work. Only when he hurt his back and had to have an operation did he take time from his job. He was an excellent carpenter. Even in the harshest weather, my father went to work.

My mother, who had a strong work ethic, started her career as a childcare teacher in her forties. She, too, seldom stayed home. Both parents were perfectly healthy into their seventies. Their children grew up knowing that they would not tolerate our wanting to stay home because we had a little head or stomach pain.

With regard to health, the focus at home was always positive. I believe they provided a powerful example about not focusing on ill health.

While I share some of my stories, think of some thoughts and beliefs you observed as a child.

1) My mother suffered during her menopause. As a young person, observing her, I decided that this was not going to be my experience. As a result, I breezed through menopause.

2) My mother went grey at a very young age. I also went grey at a very young age. I went to the hairdresser every two weeks to cover the grey. One day I made this decision - I told the universe what I wanted, stated it positively: "I want my original colour back." I trusted it was on its way, knowing it was possible. I went on with my life. I forgot my request, and did not look in the mirror to check my hairline. About a month later, my hairdresser said to me, "In all my 20 years in this trade I have never seen this before." My black hair continues to grow, even though I am in my sixties, illustrating that my body follows my mind.

3) I was my grandmother's favourite and all my relatives said I was so much like her. She was a short lady. Everyone in my family is 5 feet 4 inches or more, and my father was 6 feet 3 inches. I like being identified with my grandmother whom I loved dearly. She was only 5 feet tall and so was I until I decided I

wanted to be taller. Since then I've grown 2 inches. I am now 5 feet 2 inches tall and continue to grow taller

In the past I asked for both of these things, but nothing changed. Now I know why. Even though I wanted it, I did not believe it was possible I bought into the belief that when we grow older we grow shorter, our hair turns grey and we lose some of our vision. Now I know that does not have to be my experience.

Anything is possible if you want it bad enough. Now I am working on improving my vision to 20/20, having smooth, firm skin and a toned, lean body.

Does any of this information remind you of things you have brought into your life?

If I had said over and over again that I do not want to go through what my mother did, would that have worked? No, because I was talking about what I did not want, rather than what I want. I was saying no to the universe. What I resist, persists.

I) I HAD TO ASK FOR WHAT I WANTED.

2) TAKE MY ATTENTION OFF OF THE PROBLEM.

3) FEEL GOOD WHILE I WAITED FOR THE UNIVERSE TO GIVE IT TO ME.

4) AND THE LAST AND THE MOST DIFFICULT: TO BELIEVE THAT WHAT WE ARE ASKING FOR IS ON ITS WAY AND THAT IT WAS POSSIBLE TO HAVE IT.

How strong is your desire to have what you say you want?

Exercises To Assist You:

1) CREATE A LIST OF THE THINGS YOU NOW WANT IN YOUR LIFE ABOUT YOUR HEALTH, BODY AND YOURSELF.

2) WRITE PAGES AND PAGES OF STATEMENTS APPRECIATING YOURSELF AND APPRECIATING YOUR BODY.

3) STAND IN FRONT OF THE MIRROR NAKED AND APPRECIATE ALL THE PARTS OF YOU

4) REMEMBER A TIME WHEN YOU WERE THE PERFECT WEIGHT OR SIZE. OR SOMEONE YOU ADMIRE WHO HAS THE BODY, BEAUTY AND VITALITY YOU WANT.

6) START PUTTING THAT SMILE ON YOUR FACE AND WATCH HOW THE BODY WIL FOLLOW HOW YOU FEEL.

ALWAYS HOLD THE IMAGE OF THE WAY YOU WOULD LIKE TO BE AND THE BODY WILL FOLLOW.

I hold a picture of myself when I was 17 years old. In my mind I was the perfect weight, healthy with shiny hair and a smooth clear complexion I experience the feelings of appreciation for my health and vitality. I know I will never be 17 years old again, but I can feel as good as I did then.

YOUR LIFE IS NOW!

Not tomorrow when you will be the perfect weight, you have to be happy about it NOW!

Carrie's Story

Carrie grew up in a very negative home where both parents were very negative about themselves and others who were fat. Because of their habits, she learned her negative thinking at a very young age. She learned to hate her body because she was overweight. This is not to blame her parents, because they only taught her what they had learned from their parents. Only when she was able to overcome their influence and create her own positive life did things change for her.

Some of us do not feel worthy of having good things, but only we can break the evil spell and remind ourselves that OUR POWER IS IN THE NOW.

By this, I mean RIGHT NOW WHERE YOU ARE STANDING YOU CAN EITHER CONTINUE TO FEEL THE WAY YOU ARE FEELING about yourself and your body, OR YOU CAN DECIDE to speak and feel more positively about yourself. Right now, what can you turn your attention to in order to make yourself feel good? Your hands, your hair, your smile? Pick one, and start feeling good about it NOW!

Exercise

1) Stand in front of a mirror naked and focus on your good points and the parts of your body that make you feel good.

2) Most times we have 20 good things about our body we like, and maybe one or two things we do not like. But most of us focus on those two things and then everything else about the body follows those negative feelings.

3) IGNORE THE BAD, FOCUS ONLY ON THE GOOD.

4) Remember the times when you felt good about yourself as a person or some things you did that made you feel good.

5) Remember times when your body felt strong and energized. You were glowing with perfect health.

6) If you do not have a memory of ever feeling healthy, think of someone you know who you admire for their health and personality. See yourself as having their glow, and picture of perfect health and confidence.

For myself I use the image of Tina Turner. I told the universe I want to have her vitality, her strong body with lean firm legs, clear complexion, healthy shiny natural hair, white teeth, 20-20 vision and at least 5 feet 4 inches in height.

7) See yourself 10 years from now living a healthy fun-filled life.

8) Intend the night before that you want to wake up energized, full of life and ready for the day.

9) Spend time with children and observe their confidence, their energy, and playfulness.

In his nineties, George Bernard Shaw fell from a ladder while pruning an apple tree. Filmmaker Leni Reiffenstahl earned her scuba license when she was 76 years old. Benjamin Franklin invented, explored and influenced those around him well into his eighties.

We've bought into so many things that the media give us about aging, health and beauty. It is time to take back our power and not allow others to dictate to us.

WHICH FEELS BETTER: TO WORRY ABOUT YOUR HEALTH, HOW YOUR BODY LOOKS OR TO ENJOY THE TIMES OF YOUR LIFE WHILE YOU ARE LIVING THEM?

YOUR LIFE IS NOW, NOT TOMORROW WHEN YOU HAVE ALL THAT YOU WANT. TO GET WHAT YOU WANT TOMORROW, YOU HAVE TO BE HAPPY TODAY.

Forever Young - Healing The Body Visualization

1) Find a comfortable place to lie down, where you will not be disturbed. Turn off the phone.

   Put on some soothing music, wear comfortable loose clothes and cover yourself with a blanket if you wish. You need to feel safe and comfortable to be able to relax and fully experience this exercise.
   Breathe in and out slowly and evenly for a few breaths. As you are breathing, allow your body to relax more and more. When you breathe out allow the breath to be released out through the legs and feet. Do this by focusing your attention on the exhalation at your hips, thighs, legs and feet.

2) Now place your attention around the head. Notice if you have any tension there. Some people feel the tension. Some see images. The tension has been described as steel bands, pressure, a colour, or they just sense the constriction. Once you have identified the tension, breathe in and out a few times to release it. If it is an image you are seeing, imagine you are reaching in and grabbing that image. Then discard it outside of the body as you exhale. Notice how it disintegrates. Then look or sense to see if there is anything under what you just removed and, if so, repeat the process of grabbing the image that you see or sense and releasing it by exhaling. Notice how it disintegrates. If you do not see an image but just feel tension, then breathe out the tension.

3) Now focus on the face and repeat the some process.

4) Then go to the throat.

5) Then the shoulders arms and hands. The images here have sometimes been described as bricks or heavy sacks. The hands have been bound with rope, leather bands and chains.

6) Then the chest area front and back.

7) Then the stomach. There are many layers of stomach muscles, so make sure when you relax one layer of muscles that the layer under that is also relaxed. If not, make sure to breathe into that area and then out, to fully let go.

8) The next area is the pelvis, buttocks, and thighs. In the pelvic area, many females see images of chastity belts. When one area is released they sometimes see another belt under the one they just let go.

9) The final area is the legs, knees, ankles and feet. Many have felt or seen images of their feet stuck in cement. For some they felt or saw images of the feet bound by chains.

10) Now imagine or see the colour of indigo entering the crown. ALLOW THIS COLOUR TO MOVE THROUGH AND HEAL THE BODY.

11) Fall asleep. Just allow the mind to be soft and peaceful and feel free to return and become fully present when you wish.

DO THE MEDITATION AS OFTEN AS YOU WISH TO REJUVENATE AND HEAL THE BODY, MIND, EMOTIONS, AND TO RECONNECT WITH YOUR SOURCE.

a) Get happy, stay happy. Then the universe can bring you what you want.

b) Find anything to appreciate.

c) Decide that you want to be happy.

d) We have to become more conscious creators.

Exercise

Take your What I Want Now list regarding your health, and your list on Feeling Worthy and Loving Yourself. Read the list over again add any other statements regarding your health or wanting to feel forever young If you have placed this information on a tape you may want to play the words back to yourself. If you choose to listen to the tape you may want to get comfortable on a blanket or mat. Do whatever you need to do in order to feel safe and comfortable.

By reading your notes and/or listening to your words on the tape it helps you to move to feeling better, even before you start the visualization, and you will benefit more from the exercise.

You may also choose to go directly to the visualization if you feel you are already feeling good.

Stand in front of a mirror. For some this may be too confrontational In this case, use the visualization described above until you feel stronger and more empowered, and can use the real mirror. For those of you who are comfortable, you may want to stand naked in front of the mirror.

As you stand in front of the mirror, scan the body and allow yourself to just observe. Do not judge. Notice your eyes, your hair, your ears, your complexion, your neck, your shoulders, your arms, the chest area, your stomach, your hips and your thighs, your legs and your feet. Just notice.

How do you feel as you scanned the body? Are you pleased with what you see or did you feel disappointed? Are you excited about what is to come in regard to what you have requested for your body? How are you feeling about your body in relationship to the vision and image that you hold for your body? Do you have any judgment? See if you can get beyond the feelings of judgment. Feel good about what you see in the mirror, knowing what you are intending about your body is on its way to you. Do you feel energized or does the image reflecting back to you look tired? Are you seeing excitement in your eyes?

Are you holding your head high or are you slouching? Are you feeling comfortable looking at yourself? Look right into your eyes now and say this affirmation to yourself.

"The past no longer affects my present and my future." Repeat this to yourself a few times. Notice how much stronger you feel and how much more in touch you are starting to feel with these words.

Notice what the body does. You may observe you are now standing more erect. Holding your head even higher. You see yourself looking deeper and deeper into your eyes. You feel more comfortable and relaxed. You may be feeling a sense of invincibility and conviction. All is well in your life and no matter what comes your way in your life you can handle it.

Think about some of your past accomplishments. It does not matter how large or how small. Maybe it was a time that you passed an exam, wrote a poem, took a part in a play or wrote a book. You may be proud about the fact that you maintained this strong, youthful, healthy body. Allow yourself to feel those joyful times. Maybe you did well in your work or you are a positive creative person.

Maybe you are a good artist. Take some more time here to remember those things about yourself that makes you feel good when you are thinking about your past accomplishments. Notice how your stance has changed, as you remind yourself of how great you are.

Now tell yourself (aloud if you wish) some wonderful things about you. You are intelligent. You are a good person. You are generous and kind. You care about others (maybe a little too much sometimes) and want them to be happy. You have a good sense of humour.

As you look into your eyes tell yourself, "I am perfect just the way I am." Breathe in and out slowly three times. Allow yourself to feel the essence of those words and what they truly mean to you. You may also want to say some positive and encouraging affirmations to yourself Describe things that you like about yourself. For example, "I love the way my body follows my mind when I give it a positive image to hold," "I love how lean and strong my muscles are," or "I love my clear glowing healthy skin." Make sure you hold eye contact while continuing to say what you love and like about yourself.

You may want to tell yourself, "I am open to the possibility of having a healthy youthful body and a joyous prosperous, long fulfilling life." "I am open to the possibility of experiencing this in all areas of my life."

Continue to look directly into your eyes. You may want to tell yourself that whenever you are feeling a little insecure, that you will bring yourself back to this mirror. You will look right into your eyes and you will remind yourself of who you truly are - a powerful creator who can have what you want.

After saying these positive and empowering invocations, you may notice that you are standing taller. There is a sparkle in your eyes. Notice how you are feeling from the inside out. You have an inner strength and a love for life that radiates out to the world.

Imagine yourself walking through your day, with these feelings of assurance, feeling good about yourself. Have the sense that you can have whatever you want.

See yourself interacting with your family members, and your friends. Maybe it is in a work environment. See yourself feeling very relaxed, happy and contented. And notice that the people that you meet are feeling exactly like you.

Imagine yourself ten years from now. See yourself going through your day, and how easily your body moves. You also feel very energized, and full of life. You and others are amazed how great you look and feel. Your hair is shiny and healthy. Your skin is radiant and clear. Your body is the exact weight you like. Your muscles are strong, healthy and lean. You feel wonderful and it shows in the spring and bounce in your walk and the way you carry yourself with confidence and grace.

You feel good because finally you were willing to stop blaming outside circumstances for what was going wrong in your body and in your relationships. You were willing to let go of your past and move forward. It also pleases you that even though in the beginning it was not always easy to apply the tools, you stuck with it and had so much fun doing them. You feel invincible and now the only person that stops you is you. You tell yourself, "I now know I can have whatever I want." This pleases you.

You feel younger now than when you were in your teens. What excites you is that no matter how many more birthdays you may celebrate in the future, to you it is just a number. Now what is more important to you is to continue to feel good. You cannot wait to get up in the morning so you can watch the universe deliver to you more of what you ask for. AFFIRM TO YOURSELF, "I LOVE MY BODY, I LOVE MY LIFE."

Start coming back into the space. Bring all your feelings of courage, and conviction. Remember that sense of "I can have all this, I am deserving of all of this."

Take your time and come out of the visualization when you feel ready.

Exercises

1) Draw how well you looked and felt.

2) Write down the words you said to yourself. Paste them in a location where you will see them. (For example, on the bathroom mirror.) Or carry them with you so that you can easily reach for them when you are feeling unsure of yourself.

3) If it is too difficult to imagine yourself the way you would like to be, do anything else to feel good.

4) Cut out pictures from magazines of the new you that you envisioned. Place them on a bristol board, in a box or scrapbook. Some people label and call these objects their attraction/treasure or creation places. This means that whatever they want to manifest and bring into their lives, they place in or on these objects.

5) Find anything to appreciate.

6) Do simple things for yourself such as taking a walk in the park. (It does not have to cost money.) Write an appreciative note to yourself. Take a nice bath. Paint your toenails. Light some candles. Have a simple meal, do your nails, draw, paint, dance, sing.

7) Take a "leap of faith," meaning be willing to believe it is possible before you see the manifestation.

8) Start putting that smile on your face, and watch how your body will follow how you feel.

9) Cut pictures of people you admire for their success and their inner and outer beauty.

10) Write positive things about the different parts of your body.

11) Write in a journal how you are feeling about yourself now.

12) Cut out pictures from magazines of people you admire for their inner beauty and youthfulness and place them in your dream book, or on you board or in your treasure box.

---

waterfall visualization

Find a comfortable place to sit or lie down. You may want to play some soothing music. You may cover yourself with a blanket, if you wish. Allow yourself to relax more and more. Allow the body to relax and let go of any of the day's concerns. Take in a few deep breaths. On the exhalation, let go more and more of any tension you may be holding onto. Inhale again and when you exhale notice the breath moving through the abdomen area, down through the thighs, through the calves and all the way out through your feet. Now allow your breath to find its own rhythm, feeling more and more relaxed.

Now imagine yourself standing under a waterfall. The water temperature is just the way you like it. There are beautiful tall trees. The falls are surrounded by lush foliage, colourful flowers and the smell and the freshness of the water. Feel the strength of the cliffs and the surrounding mountains. The view and the beauty of the waterfall is breathtaking. All you hear is the sound of the water flowing, and birds singing. Allow this water to cascade over your body as you imagine all fatigue, pain or any emotional challenges you may have leave your body. You relax and allow more and more. You are feeling more and more refreshed and energized. Your fatigue and concerns are starting to wash away into the river.

Now ask your body what colour it needs. Choose from the 7 primary chakra colours which are red, orange, yellow, green, blue, indigo and violet. Once you have your answer, imagine the waterfall now turning that colour and washing all over you. Trust that whatever word, picture or feeling that came to you was the perfect colour for you. Breathe in the colour. Feel the healing power of the colour. You are feeling more and more refreshed. You feel your youth, and passion for life returning once more. Your confidence, optimistic and feeling of invincibility are also returning. You thank yourself for taking this time to rejuvenate and refresh.

When you feel complete with the colour you choose, you may want to ask your body what other colour it needs and allow that colour to wash over you until you feel complete and satisfied.

Exercises

Write about how you felt when you allowed the stress of the day to leave your body and calm your emotions.

Write about how you felt when the colour you chose made you feel better.

1) For those of you who draw, you may want to draw what you imagined about the beauty of the falls. You can place this picture in a place where you meditate or where you spend a lot of time. The picture will act as a catalyst to remind you of your eternal health and beauty.

2) You may want to promise yourself that whenever you are feeling stressed, you will bring yourself back to this waterfall.

Items to Remember:

a) Get happy and stay happy. Then your source can bring you what you want

b) Find anything to appreciate.

c) Decide that you want to be happy.

d) Become more aware of the thoughts you hold about your body and yourself.

e) Do simple things for yourself to feel good.

f) Take that "leap of faith." Be willing to believe it is possible before you see the manifestation.

g) Start putting that smile on your face and watch how your body will follow you.

Students comments

"I also notice when my intentions are pure, healing comes into family situations. When I am feeling good, I have more vitality, I send out good feelings to people around me, more smiles are given and received and my face has a glow that is notice by people. I have had set backs when I let go of the teachings and I see changes in my vibration and people around me. Now that I know the difference I am glad to put this practise into my daily life. I am new at this and I intend to come to a point in my life where it is my second skin. Thank you for your kindness, Marlene. You are wonderful." K.S.

"These strategies have brought me overflowing joy. I have never been this happy. I now look in the mirror and appreciate my positive aspects, accept my body, love it unconditionally, and feel beautiful and youthful inside and out. I know that my body is now healing itself, as I am the creator of my own experience. I have an autistic child, who has never felt comfortable in clothes, and has refused to wear anything around home. Now that I am so joyful, accepting my body, she has chosen to start wearing clothes at home. We are becoming closer. I feel excited, more inspired, healthy, and empowered. Thank you Marlene for helping me to see that I can make my dreams come true." M T

Sypnopsis

You can have the body, health and vitality that you want. All you have to do is practice seeing yourself looking wonderful, and feeling great. You will begin to attract experiences and people who will assist you in reaching your goals to feel healthier and look more youthful. Practice appreciating yourself each time you look in the mirror by affirming the things that you love about yourself.

As you ask and appreciate yourself, you will be astonished at how much comes your way. Appreciate your body by affirming that you believe in the power of healing. See your cells repairing themselves, becoming stronger, energized and youthful again. Quiet your mind each day so that you can listen to your inner guidance system which will help you feel and look great.

The peace and understanding you bring to yourself will reflect outwardly on the world around you. Do not consider it selfish to feel good about yourself, because by doing so you create a better world for everyone.

Nine Principles For Joyous Living

Joyous living skill #1:the present principle. Your life is now, now is the time to live it!

Joyous living skill #2: stay joyful, trust your higher self to guide you to the things you want!

Joyous living skill #3: stop looking into others' eyes for validation. This is your life and you get to choose how you want to feel.

Joyous living skill #4: our fear is our higher self telling us that what we fear, we desire to change.

Joyous living skill # 5: right now you have the power to create a better relationship. Get happy, and you will have a happy relationship.

Joyous living skill #6: be willing to own your own part in your relationships. There is no need to forgive.

Joyous living skill #7: tell your body what you want in the positive, and your body will oblige.

Joyous living skill #8: it is your birthright to have success. Believe it is possible. The universe will bring it to you. Let's get started!

Joyous living skill #9: smile more! Laugh more! Dance more! And your body will mirror that back to you!

Recommended Reading

Abraham-Hicks Publications www.abraham-hicks.com <http://www.abraham-hicks.com/>

Bristol, Claude M "The Magic Of Believing"

Dyer, Wayne "When you believe it you will see it", "The Power of Intention"

Hay, Louise L " You Can Heal Your Life."

Hill, Napoleon. "Think and Grow Rich."

Jung Carl Gustav. www.amazonbooks.com <http://www.amazonbooks.com/>

Seigal,Bernie M.D "Prescriptions for Living"

Troward, Thomas "How to use the Mental Science to live the life you have only dreamed of."

Walsh, Neale Donald. "Conversations With God."

Wattles, Wallace D. "The Science of Getting Rich" www.WallacedWattles.com <http://www.wallacedwattles.com/>

Williamson, Marrianne "Everyday grace, Having hope, Finding Forgiveness, and Making Miracles"

The Course In Miracles www.courseinmiracles.com <http://www.courseinmiracles.com/>

ISBN 141202311-4

9 781412 023115